Improving Healthcare Operations

Sharon J Williams

Improving Healthcare Operations

The Application of Lean, Agile and Leagility in Care Pathway Design

palgrave
macmillan

Sharon J Williams
College of Human & Health Sciences
Swansea University
Swansea, United Kingdom

ISBN 978-3-319-46912-6   ISBN 978-3-319-46913-3 (eBook)
DOI 10.1007/978-3-319-46913-3

Library of Congress Control Number: 2016953103

© The Editor(s) (if applicable) and the Author(s) 2017
This work is subject to copyright. All rights are solely and exclusively licensed by the Publisher, whether the whole or part of the material is concerned, specifically the rights of translation, reprinting, reuse of illustrations, recitation, broadcasting, reproduction on microfilms or in any other physical way, and transmission or information storage and retrieval, electronic adaptation, computer software, or by similar or dissimilar methodology now known or hereafter developed.
The use of general descriptive names, registered names, trademarks, service marks, etc. in this publication does not imply, even in the absence of a specific statement, that such names are exempt from the relevant protective laws and regulations and therefore free for general use.
The publisher, the authors and the editors are safe to assume that the advice and information in this book are believed to be true and accurate at the date of publication. Neither the publisher nor the authors or the editors give a warranty, express or implied, with respect to the material contained herein or for any errors or omissions that may have been made.

Cover illustration: Abstract Bricks and Shadows © Stephen Bonk/Fotolia.co.uk

Printed on acid-free paper

This Palgrave Macmillan imprint is published by Springer Nature
The registered company is Springer International Publishing AG
The registered company address is: Gewerbestrasse 11, 6330 Cham, Switzerland

Dedicated to Patricia

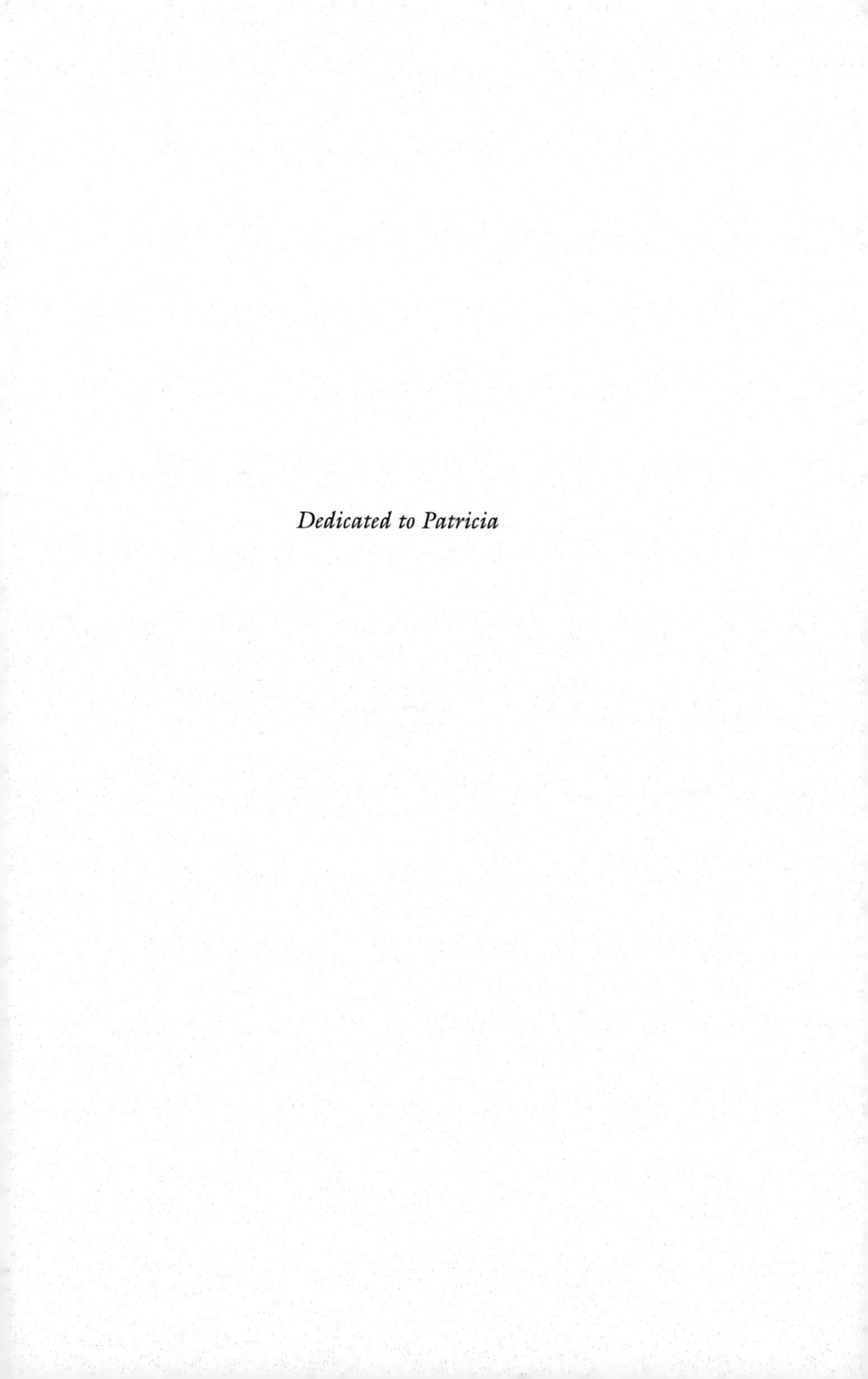

Acknowledgements

The author would like to thank all the patients, relatives, healthcare professionals and managers that took part in this study. This study was funded by the Health Foundation as part of the author's improvement science fellowship. Without either of these this study would not have been possible. This research was inspired by the late Professor Denis Towill, Cardiff Business School, Cardiff University, to whom the author is most grateful and saddened he did not see the final manuscript. The author would also like to thank Dr Lynne Caley, Professor Pauline Found and Phillip Williams for reading the early draft chapters and Madeleine Holder and Liz Barlow who commissioned this work and provided guidance and support when bringing together the final manuscript.

CONTENTS

1 Healthcare Systems in the Twenty-first Century 1

2 Improving Healthcare Systems 15

3 Lean in Healthcare 29

4 Delivering Agile and Person-centred Care 45

5 Leanness Plus Agility = Leagility 57

6 Methodology 69

7 Analysis of the COPD Pathway: Lean, Agile and Leagility 79

8 Analysis of the Huntington's Disease Pathway: Lean, Agility and Leagility 95

9 Discussion and Theoretical Reflections	107
10 Conclusion and Future Research Agenda	121
Index	133

List of Abbreviations

A&E	Accident & Emergency Dept. (also known as ED)
BLF	British Lung Foundation
CCG	Clinical Commissioning Group
COPD	Chronic Obstructive Pulmonary Disease
DP	Decoupling Point
HD	Huntington's Disease
HDA	Huntington's Disease Association
ICP	Integrated care pathway
IDP	Information Decoupling Point
MDP	Material Decoupling Point
MDT	Multidisciplinary team
PCC	Person-centred care
PDP	Patient Decoupling Point
QI	Quality improvement
R&D	Research and Development
RRS	Runners, repeaters and strangers
SCM	Supply chain management

List of Figures

Fig. 1.1	Concept of a "joined-up", patient-centred healthcare system	5
Fig. 1.2	Theoretical framework	6
Fig. 2.1	Seamless healthcare supply system	20
Fig. 2.2	Actioning the systems approach in seamless healthcare delivery system	21
Fig. 4.1	Distinguishing attributes of lean and agile supply	49
Fig. 4.2	Distinguishing attributes of lean healthcare and agile healthcare supply	50
Fig. 4.3	Model for improvement	53
Fig. 5.1	Lean, agile or leagile? Matching your supply chain to the marketplace	59
Fig. 5.2	Supply chain strategies and positioning of decoupling points	61
Fig. 5.3	Conceptual model: Leagility in the design and integration of healthcare systems	65
Fig. 7.1	High level of process map of COPD patient pathway	82
Fig. 7.2	Proposed use of the DP in a sub-COPD process—respiratory clinic	84
Fig. 7.3	Example of an emotion map for patients	91
Fig. 7.4	Example of an emotion map for staff	92
Fig. 8.1	High level of map of HD patient pathway	98
Fig. 8.2	Back-office and front-office decoupling point for HD pathway	100
Fig. 9.1	Distinguishing lean, agile and leagility attributes of the COPD pathway	111
Fig. 9.2	Distinguishing lean, agile and leagility attributes of the HD pathway	112
Fig. 9.3	Patient pathways and positioning of decoupling points	113

Fig. 10.1　Seamless healthcare system　124
Fig. 10.2　Revised conceptual model for seamless healthcare system　128

List of Tables

Table 3.1	Key assumptions of lean thinking	31
Table 3.2	Typology of lean implementation in England NHS hospitals	32
Table 4.1	Characteristics of agile manufacturing and agile healthcare	47
Table 4.2	Combining the PDSA cycle and agile methodology	54
Table 5.1	Supply chain strategies and healthcare examples	63
Table 6.1	Inclusion and exclusion criteria for the selection of research participants	72
Table 6.2	Extract from the thematic framework	75
Table 6.3	Criteria and strategies employed to demonstrate credibility of research	75
Table 7.1	Key enablers and inhibitors of patient flow in the COPD pathway	86
Table 7.2	Factors inhibiting information flows in the COPD pathway	87
Table 7.3	Factors enabling information flows in the COPD pathway	87
Table 9.1	Attributes of COPD and HD pathways	109

CHAPTER 1

Healthcare Systems in the Twenty-first Century

Abstract This chapter sets the context for this study by examining the challenges that beset global healthcare systems and the National Health Service (NHS) in the UK. The problems arising in healthcare operations management are described along with a brief outline of quality improvement (QI) programmes in the UK. Key theories and concepts employed within the study are defined; these include: lean, agile, agility, supply chain management (SCM), systems thinking and quality improvement (QI). A summary of the study is provided which aims to examine the (re)design of two patient pathways employing lean and agile approaches.

Keywords Global healthcare system · NHS · Quality Improvement · Lean

Introduction

This introductory chapter sets the context of the study in relation to global healthcare systems and then more specifically in relation to the NHS in the UK. The content and structure of the study are unpacked. Some key definitions and a brief outline of the study are provided. The concluding section of the chapter summarises the discussion and provides an overview of the following chapters.

The Context: Global Healthcare

Healthcare organisations globally continue to struggle with managing increasing demands for their services with limited or shrinking resources. To respond to what has been termed the triple challenge of demographic pressures, a changing burden of disease, and rising patient and public expectations organisations are aware that they have to do something different in the way they organise themselves and function in order to provide the level and quality of care that is expected by patients (Burgess and Radnor 2012).

Projected demographic shifts and societal changes are expected to intensify the pressure on health systems and demand new and improved ways of delivering healthcare. Ageing populations in both emerging and developed nations are increasing the demand for healthcare. According to the United Nations, the world's population is expected to increase by one billion people by 2025 (United Nations Population Fund 2013). Of that billion, 300 million will be people aged 65 or older, as globally life expectancy continues to rise. Additional healthcare resources and service innovation are needed to support this increase. Different parts of the world will be impacted differently by these demographic changes. Successful and sustainable change will require flexible and adaptive models to fit the new health economies.

As the population grows, technological innovations in assistive technology and mobile healthcare are expected to advance cost-effective health solutions. Technology and analytics are providing new ways of promoting wellness, preventing disease and providing person-centred care. With these changes comes the need for more effective partnerships between the public and private sectors. Collaborations that in the past may have seemed unlikely will need to become commonplace.

Running in parallel to this growth for demand are the austerity measures which are likely to affect the supply and delivery of services. Such measures will demand a rethink in the way that services are delivered which often translates to doing more with the same or less resources. It is therefore clear that practices need to change in order for these challenges to be met. For some time, we have seen improvement approaches and technologies which have originated and matured in other sectors being used to improve the delivery of healthcare. Although we have seen some positive results, some organisations have struggled to make and/or sustain improvements. As we see many more patients coping with complex and multiple conditions, what is becoming apparent is the need for a much more integrated approach to the way we(re) design healthcare services and the approaches we use to improve them. It is unclear currently how different improvement technologies can be aligned to ensure that improvement is maximised and the possibility of sub-optimising parts of the healthcare system is avoided.

The Context—UK Healthcare

Like other healthcare systems, the NHS in the UK is under pressure from rising deficits, worsening performance and declining staff morale. This means that the NHS, a public healthcare system which is free at the point of use, is facing its biggest challenges for many years, whilst at the same time pressures on social care are escalating (The King's Fund 2015). The NHS Five Year Forward View (NHS England 2014) estimates that the NHS needs additional funding of £8 billion a year by 2020/21 and this projection depends on delivering efficiency savings of £22 billion a year by 2020/21. This has been described as hugely ambitious and requires much higher productivity improvements than the NHS has historically been able to deliver.

UK governments traditionally have relied on external pressures such as targets, inspection and competition to drive reform and improvements. This approach has delivered mixed results. If we examine the experience of some high-performing health systems in the UK and internationally it suggests that organisations, in their pursuit to transform care, should ensure continuity of leadership, engaging staff and focusing on a clear commitment to put patients first (The King's Fund 2015). NHS England has recently taken steps to relax the key waiting time targets for more than 50 hospitals in England to help ease their financial problems. The move is part of a package of measures taken by NHS England after hospitals exceeded their budgets by a record amount in 2015. Some of the fines for missing targets have been removed altogether (e.g. A&E, cancer and routine operations). A new regime is being set up for the worst performing trusts which will include the installation of senior managers to help devise rescue plans (Triggle 2016).

The UK think tank, the King's Fund, has called for a greater emphasis to be placed on how services need to change, the starting point being new models of care proposed in the NHS Five Year Forward View. This means a shift to providing more care in the community and having better joined-up services to better meet the needs of the ageing population and the increasing number of people with long-term conditions (The King's Fund 2015). It is this call for better joined-up services that this study aims to inform. Here at a high-level supply chain perspective we visualise what a "joined up", patient-centred healthcare system might look like (see Fig. 1.1).

Healthcare Operations Management

Improving and managing healthcare operations is fundamental to the performance of individual healthcare organisations and the wider healthcare system. Within the discipline of service operations management Chase and Apte (2007) propose the following three areas of research:

- adaption of manufacturing concepts to service environments;
- frameworks for service (re)design and management; and
- tools and techniques of service operations to improve the performance in services.

To enable improvement in the delivery of service operations Maguire (2012) states the need for an effective combination and integration of people, process and technology at an organisation and system level (supply chain). Pagell (2004) highlights researching the aforementioned can be problematic but essential as the lack of integration can have a negative impact on levels of organisational performance and inter-organisational collaboration (Chan 2007).

The problems arising in healthcare operations management are described as being similar to the traditional problems in operations management including strategic planning problems (e.g. design of services), design of healthcare supply chains, facility planning and design (e.g. layout of hospitals) demand and capacity management and scheduling and workforce planning (Brandeau et al. 2004). Specific studies that have examined some of these areas include managing demand and capacity (Walley et al. 2006a); developing performance measurement systems (Walley et al. 2006b); and improving the design and delivery of healthcare processes and systems (Burgess and Radnor 2012; LaGanga 2011; De Mast et al. 2011). A more

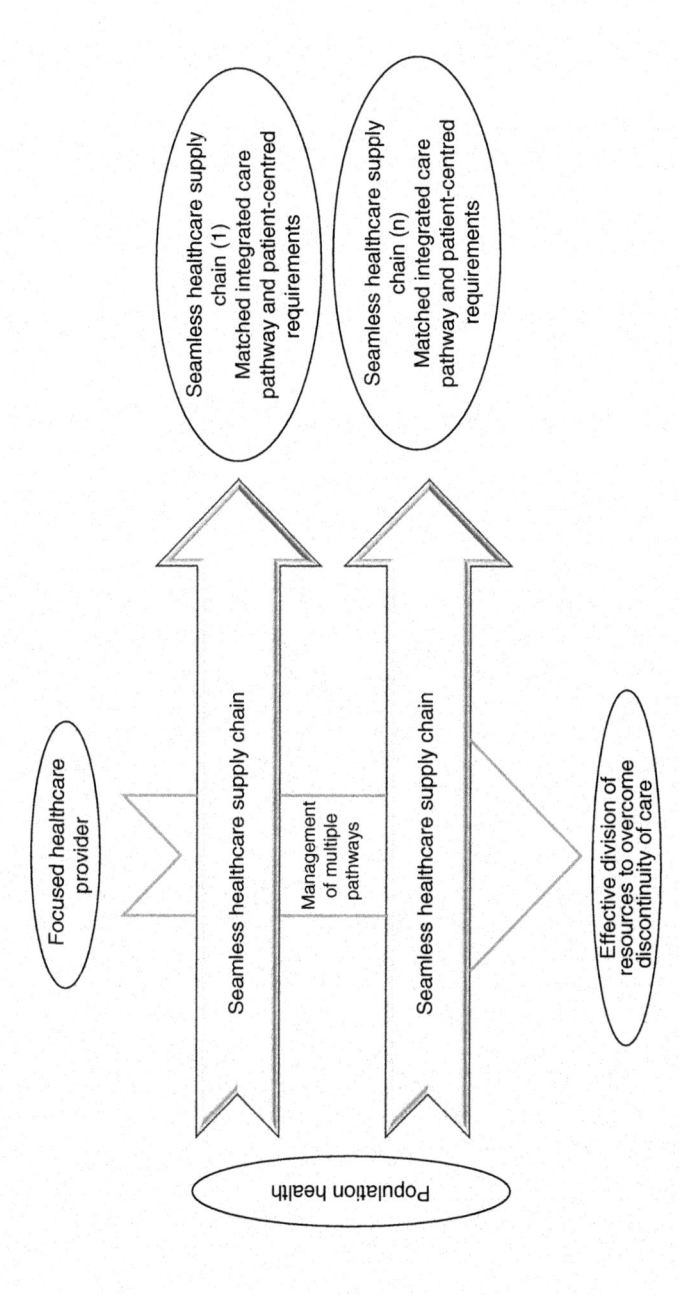

Fig. 1.1 Concept of a "joined-up", patient-centred healthcare system. (*Source*: Author)

recent addition to academic writings has been the introduction of leagility and the importance of a decoupling point (Rahimnia and Moghadasian 2010). This is one area that will be explored further within this study.

Although similar problems arise, healthcare systems and processes are reported as being more complicated than traditional manufacturing processes (Guven-Uslu et al. 2014). It is the uncertainty around patient demand, clinicians' time, availability of equipment and usage of medicine that beset decision-making and operational performance. Misaligned incentives and targets are also defined as being a barrier to implementing operations management and improvement practices in healthcare organisations (McKone-Sweet et al. 2005).

Quality Improvement and the NHS

The UK healthcare system has seen considerable investment in national improvement programmes. A full review of these is beyond the scope of this study; however, it seems appropriate to mention some of the key programmes which are still in being or evident in practice. The productive series is a well-known improvement programme which started with Productive Ward and moved to other key areas of the healthcare system including theatres, mental health and general practitioner (GP) practices. This programme was initiated by the former NHS Institute for Innovation and Improvement in 2007. The approach is based on lean principles, one of the methods examined in this text. Other programmes similar to the productive series have been employed within the UK including Transforming Care and Transforming Care at the Bedside.

There is evidence of other approaches employed within the UK. For example, Public Health Wales hosts 1,000 Lives Plus and the Prudent Healthcare campaign. The NHS Scotland Improvement Hub has a 2020 quality framework for quality, efficiency and value. The Regulation and Quality Improvement Authority is Northern Ireland's independent health and social care regulator, which encourages continuous improvement in the quality of health and social care services through a programme of inspections and reviews. For further details of the four healthcare systems in the UK see a comparative analysis commissioned by the Health Foundation (Bevan et al. 2014).

Although this study does not focus on the above national programmes it is useful to mention them here in terms of the wider context of quality improvement in healthcare and the attention it is receiving.

These programmes are helping to build the improvement capacity and capability at a national, regional and local level. This study is located at a local level with the unit of analysis being the patient pathway.

Outline of the Study

Given our discussion around healthcare operations and quality improvement we have theoretically framed the study within the context three different lenses: supply chain management; systems thinking; and quality improvement (see Fig. 1.2). In Chap. 2 we briefly review each of these within the context of the study. Given the holistic approach associated with all three lenses we see there are potential synergies that we will explore later within the text.

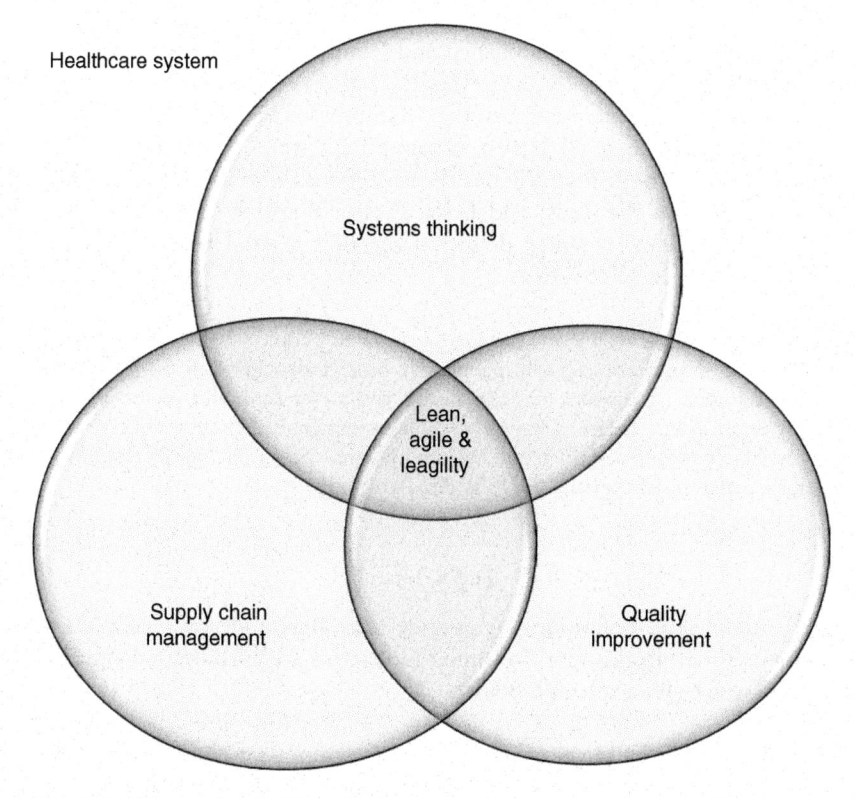

Fig. 1.2 Theoretical framework. (*Source*: Author)

The overall aim of this study is to examine how two concepts, largely associated with manufacturing, can be employed in the (re)design of patient pathways. Lean thinking has been a popular concept in healthcare since the early 2000s, whereas, agility has received limited attention and application. Here we investigate why this might be the case and try to identify the enablers and inhibitors to both approaches. In addition, we consider whether, as in manufacturing, it is possible to combine the approaches. Again, we try to identify what this might look like in terms of the two care pathways which we have studied—chronic obstructive pulmonary disease (COPD) and Huntington's disease (HD). The study has been undertaken in England and Wales. The structure and delivery of healthcare services are different in these two parts of the UK. In England, the Health and Social Care Act (2012) paved the way for reforms to how patient care in the English NHS is organised, managed and delivered. Primary Care Trusts were abolished and Clinical Commissioning Groups were introduced.

In Wales the reorganisation of the NHS came into effect on 1 October 2009 when single local health organisations were created which are responsible for delivering all healthcare services within a geographical area, rather than the Trust and Local Health Board system that existed previously. Services are now delivered through seven University Health Boards and three NHS Trusts.

> There is a desire to provide more care closer to people's homes and more self-care programmes to help people live more independent lives, provide more joined up services between health and social care, and increasingly focus on public health, creating a wellness service, rather than a sickness service. It means a shift in the balance of care, looking at whole systems rather than just hospitals. (NHS Wales 2016, np)

Definitions

We present brief definitions to provide clarity around some of the key terms used within this text. In some cases, terms are used interchangeably and these are also explained below:

- *Supply chain management* (SCM)—refers to a chain or network of organisations making and delivering a product or service (e.g. from concept to consumption). For a product-related supply chain this would usually include the management of material, information and financial flows. In terms of healthcare we propose the care supply chain incorporates pre-diagnosis to post-diagnosis including management of preventative and long-term care. As we explore here the flows are likely to include patients, materials, information and emotions.

- *Quality improvement* (QI)—a simple definition refers to a systematic and sustainable approach that uses specific techniques to improve quality. In terms of healthcare, "improving quality is about making healthcare safe, effective, patient-centred, timely, efficient and equitable" (The Health Foundation 2013). QI can be discussed in relation to specific approaches such as lean and Six Sigma. Other terms such as continuous improvement and improvement science are used interchangeably with QI.
- *Systems thinking*—is seeing how things are related and connected to each other within some notion of a whole entity (Peters 2014). Feedback loops are essential to the learning and problem solving required for systems thinking. In terms of improvement it is important to understand where the boundaries lie for the system e.g. organisation, secondary care, primary care, pathway and how these might interact with any other (sub) systems.
- *Patient care pathway*—this term is used to describe the entire or part journey a patient might experience when diagnosed with a health condition, for example from pre-diagnosis which might involve seeking assistance from a GP, through to diagnosis, to post-diagnosis including care management in the community. Often in healthcare this might be referred to as a patient journey, patient trajectory and patient pathway. In some instances, an integrated care pathway might be a term used to describe and document a patient pathway; we provide more detail of this term in Chap.6. In supply chain terms a care pathway can also be referred to as a value stream or care supply chain.
- *Lean*—refers to lean thinking as first defined by Womack and Jones (1996) and its five key principles—understanding customer (patient) value, defining the value stream (patient pathways), removing waste to improve flow, pulling resources as needed by the customer (patient) and continually striving for perfection. In Chap. 3 we explore how these principles have been adopted for a healthcare environment.

- *Agility* (also referred to as agile or agile manufacturing)—here we draw on the well-known definition from Christopher (2000, p. 37) which describes agility as
  - *"a business-wide capability that embraces organisational structures, information systems, logistics processes and, in particular, mind-sets. A key characteristic of an Agile organisation is flexibility."*

    Later in the text we make reference to the agile methodology usually seen in IT, which is a defined approach to managing software projects. This is considered mainly in light of future research and agile project planning.
- *Leagility* (also referred to as leagile)—we draw on the original definition of leagility which utilises the decoupling point to separate the part of the supply chain that operates on a forecasted and relatively predictable plan (lean), from the part of the supply chain which responds to real and unpredictable demand (agile), (Naim and Gosling 2011). In the text we explore how this concept can be employed within the (re)desigin of patient pathways.

Conclusions

This chapter has highlighted the contextual challenges that universal healthcare systems are facing. Never has there been a better time in which to examine in detail how improvement paradigms might be employed and integrated to enable better patient outcomes and improved pathway design. For example, the desire in the UK healthcare service to move care from secondary to primary care services is likely to require a whole systems view of the service.

The unit of analysis for this research project is the entire pathway from (pre)diagnosis to the management of care. This holistic view is timely and provides a useful and impactful contribution to understanding how services need to be designed in order to deliver a (joined-up) seamless and high-quality experience for patients and their carers/relatives.

Here we have briefly examined an emerging discipline of healthcare operations management and defined the key terms related to this study. In this text we explore how two concepts, lean and agile, can be used to examine the architecture and design of patient pathways.

Structure of the Publication

The structure of this publication is as follows: Chapter 2 provides an overview of three theoretical lenses relevant to this research: SCM, systems thinking and QI literature within healthcare. Chapter 3 provides specific details of implementing lean in healthcare, an approach drawn from these three areas of work. Although a systematic review is out of scope the chapter identifies themes that have emerged from the literature and considers the merits and challenges associated with the implementation of lean. Chapter 4 examines the origins of agility and its application in relation to pathway design. Chapter 5 extends the discussion to leagility, an approach which looks for the synergies between leanness and agile. Chapter 6 presents details of the methodology employed for the study. This chapter also outlines the two clinical conditions focal to the study. Chapter 7 is the first part of the analysis. This focuses on the COPD case and provides a high-level map of the patient pathway and considers where lean and agility might be used in order to improve patient, information and emotional flows. Chapter 8 examines the second case, Huntington's disease, and again provides an overview of the patient pathway and considers the role of the broker. Chapter 9 provides a deeper discussion of the results in relation to previous literature and in particular considers what learning can be transferred and adapted from operations management and SCM to healthcare. The final chapter considers the implications of this research for healthcare practitioners, academics and policy makers. In addition, we identify a future research agenda to encourage cross-disciplinary research that will help to improve healthcare systems.

REFERENCES

Bevan, G., Karanikolos, M., Exley, J., Nolte, E., Connolly, S., & Mays, N. (2014). *The four health systems in the United Kingdom: How do they compare.* London: Health Foundation. Available at http://www.health.org.uk/publication/four-health-systems-united-kingdom-how-do-they-compare [Accessed July 22, 2016].

Brandeau, M., Sainfort, F., & Pierskalla, W. (2004). Health care delivery: Current problems and future challenges. In M. Brandeau, F. Sainfort, & W. Pierskalla (Eds.), *Operations research and health care: A handbook of methods and applications.* Massachusetts: Kluwer Academic Publishers.

Burgess, N., & Radnor, Z. (2012). Service improvement in the English National Health Service: Complexities and tensions. *Journal of Management and Organisation, 18*(5), 594–607.

Chan, H. (2007). A pro-active and collaborative approach to reverse logistics – a case study. *Production Planning & Control*, *18*(4), 350–360.
Chase, R. B., & Apte, U. M. (2007). A history of research in service operations: What's the big idea? *Journal of Operations Management*, *25*(2), 375–386.
Christopher, M. (2000). The agile supply chain: Competing in volatile markets. *Industrial Marketing Management*, *29*(1), 37–44.
De Mast, J., Kemper, B., Does, R., Mandjes, M., & Van Der Bijl, Y. (2011). Process improvement in healthcare: Overall resource efficiency. *Quality and Reliability Engineering International*, *27*(8), 1095–1106.
Guven-Uslu, P., Chan, H., Ijaz, S., Bak, O., Whitlow, B., & Kumar, V. (2014). In-depth study of 'decoupling point' as a reference model: An application for health service supply chain. *Production Planning & Control*, *25*(13–14), 1107–1117.
LaGanga, L. (2011). Lean service operations: Reflections and new directions for capacity expansion in outpatient clinics. *Journal of Operations Management*, *29*(5), 422–433.
Maguire, S. (2012). Editorial – special issue. *Production Planning and Control: Service Science*, *23*(7), 477–479.
McKone-Sweet, K.E., Hamilton, P., & Willias, S.B. (2005). The ailing healthcare supply chain: A prescription for change. *Journal of Supply Chain Management*, *41*(1), 4–17.
Naim, M., & Gosling, J. (2011). On leanness, agility and leagile supply chains. *International Journal of Production Economics*, *131*, 342–354.
NHS England. (2014). *Five year forward view*. London: NHS England. Available at https://www.england.nhs.uk/wp-content/uploads/2014/10/5yfv-web.pdf.
NHS Wales (2016), Written statement: NHS Reforms, NHS Wales. Available at: http://www.wales.nhs.uk/newyddion/13330 [Accessed June 20, 2016].
Pagell, M. (2004). Understanding the factors that enable and inhibit the integration of operations, purchasing and logistics. *Journal of Operations Management*, *22*(5), 459–487.
Peters, D. (2014). The application of systems thinking in health: Why use systems thinking?. *Health Research Policy and Systems*, *12*(51), 1–6.
Rahimnia, F., & Moghadasian, M. (2010). Supply chain leagility in professional services: How to apply decoupling point concept in healthcare delivery system. *Supply Chain Management: An International Journal*, *15*(1), 80–91.
The Health Foundation. (2013). *Quality improvement made simple: What everyone should know about health care quality improvement*. London: The Health Foundation.
The King's Fund. (2015). Health and social care: Three priorities for the new government. Available at: http://www.kingsfund.org.uk/projects/new-gov/three-priorities-new-government [Accessed July 9, 2016].

Triggle, N. (2016). Hospitals given green light to miss waiting time targets, BBC News, 21st July 2016. Available at http://www.bbc.co.uk/news/health-36854557 [Accessed July 22, 2016].

United Nations Population Fund. (2013). World population to increase by one billion by 2025. Available at http://www.unfpa.org/news/world-population-increase-one-billion-2025 [Accessed July 6, 2016].

Walley, P., Silvester, K., Steyn, R., & Conway, J. B. (2006a). Managing variation in demand: Lessons from the UK National Health Service. *Journal of Healthcare Management, 51*(5), 309–322.

Walley, P., Silvester, K., & Mountford, S. (2006b). Health-care process improvement decisions: A systems perspective. *International Journal of Health Care Quality Assurance, 19*(1), 93–104.

Womack, J., & Jones, D. (1996). *Lean thinking: Banish waste and create wealth in your corporation.* New York: Simon Schuster.

CHAPTER 2

Improving Healthcare Systems

Abstract Improving healthcare has been on management and organisation agendas since the 1990s. This chapter reviews three different but complementary theoretical lenses: supply chain management (SCM), systems thinking and quality improvement (QI). In relation to improvement of healthcare the results have been variable, with even the better performing organisation struggling to sustain their improvement gains. As with other industries, when improving performance, the focus tends to be at a micro level. Conversely, systems thinking and SCM encourage organisations to think in terms of the whole system or for health and social care the entire patient pathway. This chapter considers the difficulties associated with silo (bounded) interventions, tool-based approaches to improvement and the dangers of sub-optimising the system.

Keywords Quality improvement · Systems · Supply chain · Healthcare

INTRODUCTION

Improving healthcare has been on management and organisation agendas since the 1990s. This chapter builds on the previous chapter by considering three different lenses in which to consider the improvement of healthcare systems. So far the results have been variable, with even the better performing organisation struggling to sustain their improvement gains. As with other industries, when improving performance, the focus tends to be at a

© The Author(s) 2017
S.J. Williams, *Improving Healthcare Operations*,
DOI 10.1007/978-3-319-46913-3_2

micro level. Conversely, systems thinking and supply chain management (SCM) encourage organisations to think in terms of the whole system or for health and social care the entire patient pathway.

This chapter considers the difficulties associated with silo (bounded) interventions, tool-based approaches to improvement and the dangers of sub-optimising the system. Early improvement interventions in healthcare focused on point-of-care project-based improvement, which are certainly necessary but not sufficient to achieve the scale of improvement required. With the maturity of the quality improvement (QI) movement and the building of capability and capacity we should be seeing evidence of successful projects being scaled up. To make this happen there needs to be a clear trajectory of QI that helps organisations to move from a project-based mentality to that of systems thinking which would help to safeguard against local optimisation and promote whole system change (Burgess and Radnor 2013). This chapter draws on the key principles of SCM, systems thinking and QI (our three lenses) to assess how operational improvement and excellence in system design may be achieved. There is some overlap in these three lenses but there is also sufficient distinction in which each one provides a perspective which will contribute to developing our understanding of pathway design.

Supply Chain Management

Supply chain management has been a popular concept since the 1990s, when Christopher recognised competition was no longer about companies competing against each other, but it was about the performance of their entire supply chains. A supply chain can be simply defined as the alignment of organisations that make and deliver products or services to market, which also involves the final customer (Lambert et al. 1998). This probably suggests a linear arrangement in which information and material flow unidirectional. Another definition suggests a supply chain is more of a network of organisations that are involved, through upstream (i.e. supply) and downstream (i.e. distribution) linkages, in the different processes and activities that produce value in the form of products and services delivered to the ultimate consumer (Christopher 1992). In terms of healthcare we could link this to pre-diagnosis to post-diagnosis (i.e. recovery, management of long-term care or end of life).

Healthcare, like other industries, has not given SCM the detailed attention it deserves (McKone-Sweet et al. 2005; De Vries and Huijsman 2011) despite the fact that healthcare needs to ensure good service delivery, patient safety and a reduction in costs (Kelle et al. 2009), which are precisely the premises on which SCM is based. Many healthcare supply chains are reported to suffer from complex operational management problems, which are challenging to address (Byrnes 2004; Braithwaite et al. 2007; Childerhouse and Towill 2002; Jessup et al. 2010; Karvonen et al. 2004; Lee et al. 2011; Böhme et al. 2014).

Whilst the adoption of supply chain best practices is recommended (Byrnes 2004; Schneller and Smeltzer 2006; Shih et al. 2009), there is limited guidance on which intervention will be most effective for a given situation, or how to identify transferable best practices (Lee et al. 2011; McKone-Sweet et al. 2005; Mustaffa and Potter 2009; Shah et al. 2008; Spear 2005). Much attention has been given to improving the performance of material or product-related supply chain activities (e.g. Böhme et al. 2013; 2014; Childerhouse and Towill 2002; Mason-Jones and Towill 1998), which typically consider the flow of products/materials, information, finance and possibly value. Less focus has been placed on the flow of patients and the design of patient pathways.

By utilising volume and frequency classifications such as runners, repeaters and strangers (see Bicheno 2008 for a detailed discussion) healthcare professionals can attempt to coordinate and stream activities to improve the flow of value (Walley et al. 2006). However, achieving the benefits of streaming can be problematic if the patterns of demand for provision are not known or the resource needs of the patients are not recognised across the different processes or pathways (Walley 2013; Glenday 2005). This could have consequences for the design of the healthcare supply chain or patient journey. To ensure a seamless transition from one healthcare provider to the next and from one operational approach to another, organisations need to consider how to coordinate care and communicate across organisational boundaries. In the next section we explore the various types of flow which impact on supply chain performance.

Systems Thinking and Seamless Healthcare Systems

The main focus of systems thinking is seeing how things are connected to each other with some notion of a whole entity (Peters 2014). Elmaghraby (1966) describes a "system" as a collection of interacting elements that operate to achieve a common goal. Sterman (2001) argues that system thinkers need to be able to view the world as a complex system of interconnected parts and appreciate the many interrelated (positive and negative) feedback loops required to create circular relationships. Cause and effect mapping and dynamic modelling are just some of the techniques used in systems thinking.

Systems thinking is made up of the following key components (Checkland, 1999):

* The notion of the adaptive whole is central to systems thinking where the whole entity is more than the sum of its parts.
* Systems thinking has a layered structure which, for example, can refer to autonomous departments (e.g. pathology; imaging) that are part of a larger 'whole' system (e.g. hospital). Consideration needs to be given to how these parts are connected in relation to the performance of the system as a whole.
* Organisations need internal communication and control processes to understand and respond to what is happening in the wider environment.
* Feedback loops are critical to the learning and renewal of the system.

Checkland also makes the distinction between hard and soft systems. Where hard system thinking is appropriate for well-defined technical problems (e.g. in engineering and IT), soft systems thinking is more appropriate for ill-defined and 'messy' situations which involve human beings and organisational/cultural considerations.

Systems thinking was first employed to examine continuous production systems in the chemical industry (Campbell 1958) then discrete object manufacture (e.g. Ohno 1988) and then services (e.g. Böhme et al. 2014; Parnaby and Towill 2008). Academics are often looking to make connections when conducting and interpreting research, and healthcare professionals become skilled at linking an intervention with an expected or desired result. The word "system" is derived from the Greek *sunistánai*, meaning "to cause to stand together". If we consider, as noted by Checkland, that a system is a perceived whole, made up of parts that interact towards a common purpose, we recognise that the ability to perceive, and the quality of that perception, is also part of what causes a system to stand together. Systems thinking is intended to improve the quality of those perceptions of the whole, its parts and the interactions within and between levels.

Healthcare organisations usually operate autonomously due to specialisation (Meijboom et al. 2011) which often promotes a functional approach to care rather than the integrated pathway that many patients assume or need. To ensure a seamless transition from one healthcare provider to the next, organisations need to coordinate care and communicate across organisational boundaries. It's only fairly recently that this has been recognised and as a result, the interest in using industrial processes or applying QI approaches in patient care continues to grow (Young et al. 2004).

There is a need to move away from the functional silos usually seen in healthcare (Parnaby and Towill 2008) to well-defined processes to deliver high quality of care within short lead times (Aronsson et al. 2011). Typically, the patient's journey (pathway) involves the coordination of a large number of functions in terms of both time and space. This has consequences for the design of the care supply chain (or patient journey), which ultimately should be striving to deliver a seamless and integrated service. The prism model shown in Fig. 2.1 provides a suitable framework for achieving this goal. The four proposed levels are based on the work of Werr et al. (1997). The outcome is seen as a clear strategy for designing an improved healthcare delivery process capability. Parnaby and Towill (2008) strongly recommend healthcare to construct an equivalent internal learning organisation if seamless healthcare supply systems are to be developed. We propose a systems engineering approach to understanding challenges and opportunities that face healthcare organisations as they strive to provide what is often termed "joined-up care, or integrated care pathways". This may be regarded as the innovative adaptation of the "Principle of Swift and Even Flow" (Schmenner and Swink 1998) in pursuit of the "Seamless Supply Chain" (Towill 1997). The way in which healthcare is delivered can have a profound effect on patient safety, quality care, efficiency and effectiveness of process and resource utilisation.

Parnaby and Towill (2008) help us to visualise how a seamless healthcare system might operate (see Fig. 2.2). This figure documents the information and patient flows across the posited boundaries, and throughout the healthcare processes. The authors suggest the delivery system has definite boundaries with flows entering from three sides and an outsourced flow (successfully treated patients) on the other. The three inbound flows are: resources, patients-in-need and external occurrences. The latter are events (e.g. policy changes, major incidents) that tend to disturb the system's smooth running. It is necessary to ensure the proposed designs are adequately robust to cope with such disturbances.

Peters (2014) notes the "jungle of terminology" associated with systems thinking but helpfully lists the theories (e.g. social network theory, agency dependency theory, general systems theory, chaos theory), methods and

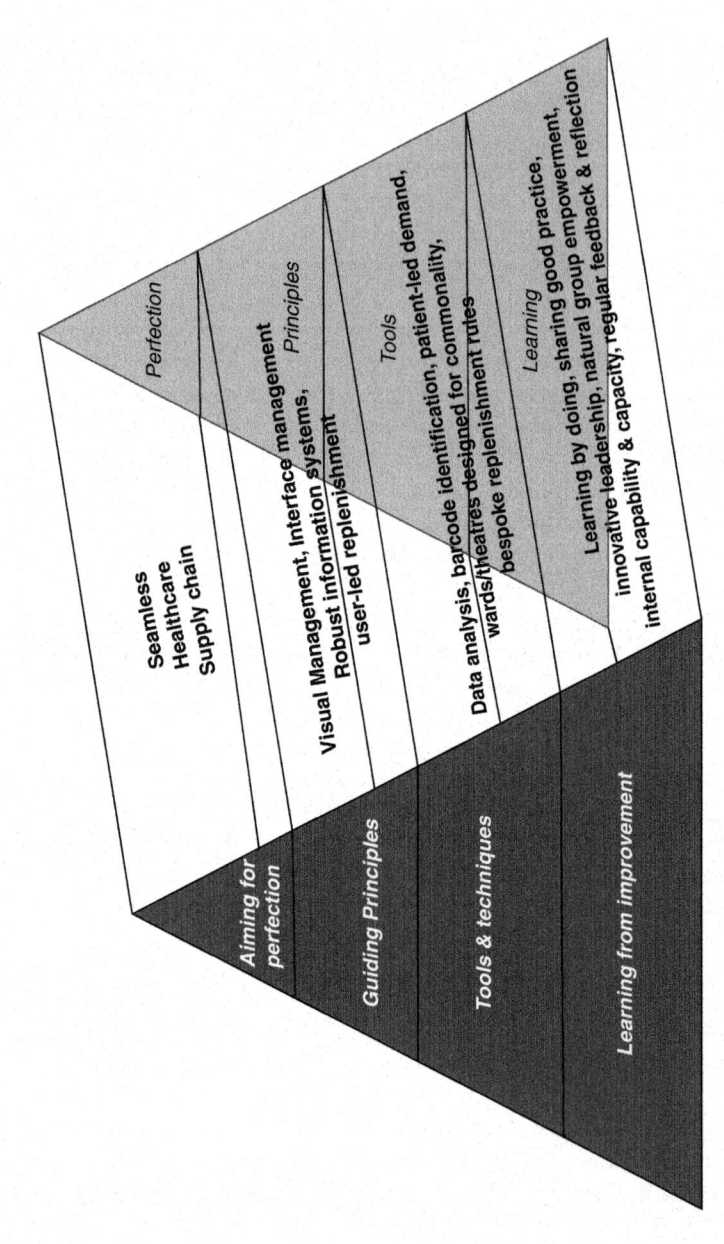

Fig. 2.1 Seamless healthcare supply system. (*Source*: Adapted from Parnaby and Towill (2008) based on Werr et al. (1997))

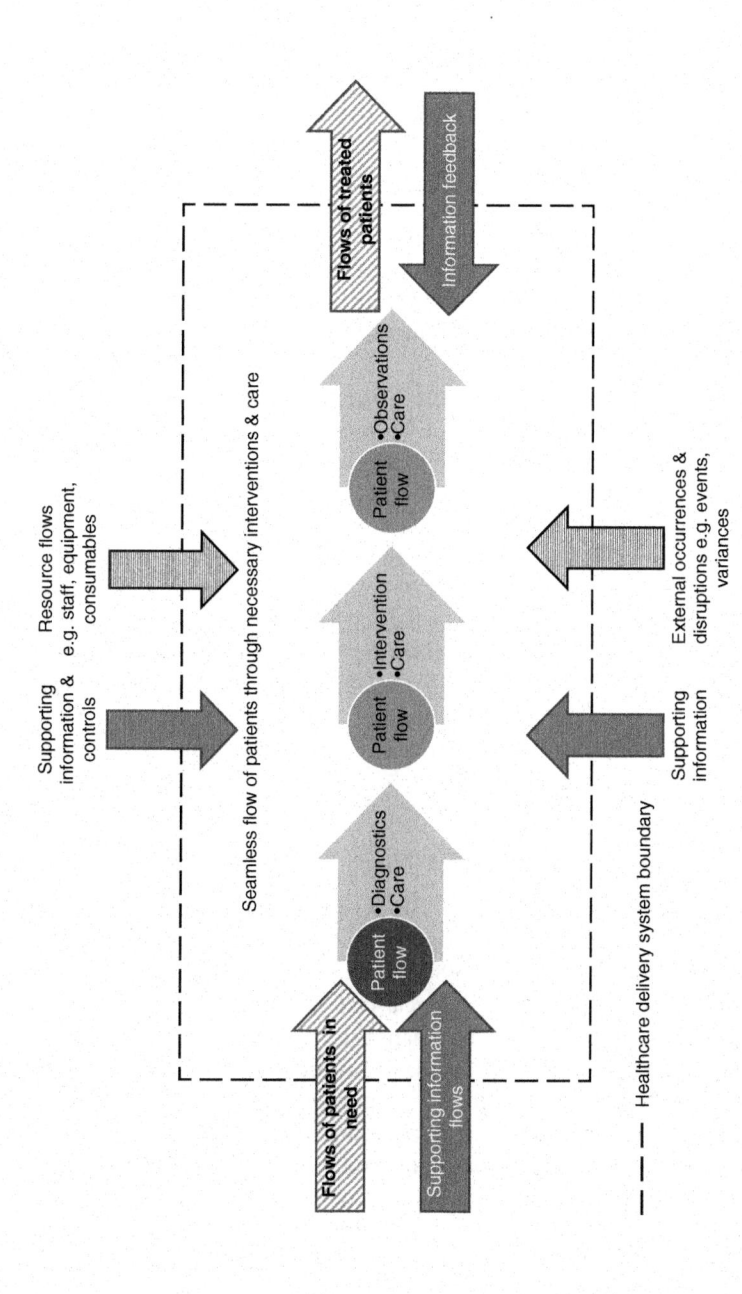

Fig. 2.2 Actioning the systems approach in seamless healthcare delivery system. (*Source*: Adapted from Parnaby and Towill (2008))

tools (e.g. process mapping, flow diagrams, service archetypes, modelling) some of which we see in use to improve healthcare systems. One notion that is prominent in systems thinking is the development and testing of "mental models" as a way of seeing the whole and to understand how things fit together. The methods and tools work in different ways to help develop such models, for example facilitating discussions (e.g. during handovers), establishing the need for more data (baseline measures for improvement or to provide feedback on performance), visualising flows and processes (e.g. visualising the patient journey), identifying bottlenecks (e.g. theatres or specialist clinics) and illustrating current and future states (e.g. for improvement and action planning).

Interest around the use of systems thinking in healthcare seems to be on the increase. One reason for its use is to inspire a scientific habit of mind (Peters 2014) and thus linking it to the current emphasis on evidence-based medicine. Systems thinking has the potential to provide opportunities to improve healthcare systems. Later in this study we use some of the systems thinking tools to form part of the analysis of the case materials.

Here we have focused very much on improving processes and systems to improve the level of integration of specialist services for the benefit of the patient. It is important to mention the need for greater involvement and input from patients in relation to managing their own healthcare needs. Later we consider the prominence of coproduction and person-centred care as mechanisms in which to engage with patients in relation to designing services around their needs.

Quality Improvement in Healthcare

Quality improvement in healthcare can be described as an approach that emphasises the better meeting of the needs of the customer (Blumenthal and Kilo 1998; Shortell et al. 1998), by focusing on work processes and systems. Berwick (1989) states that real change can only be achieved by changing the system, and by this he means the system can range from a large hospital to a small GP practice. Quality improvement has been widely adopted in healthcare, particularly in hospitals (Brennan et al. 2009). An early review of QI literature in healthcare found the determinants of success included participation of clinicians, provision of feedback to individual clinicians and a supporting organisation culture. The determinants that led to failure were described as topics/areas chosen (e.g. heart failure, chronic obstructive pulmonary disease and depression led to many implementation problems), disagreement with national guidelines on best practice and vague feedback (Shortell et al. 1998). Interestingly, the determinants of failure are mainly related to the infrastructure required to support QI rather than the approach itself (Grol et al. 2013).

The variable fidelity in the application of QI methods and the pursuit of time-based, small-scale projects are just two reasons the effectiveness of QI is mixed (Dixon-Woods and Martin, 2016). The lack of rigorous evaluation and the ability to learn from successes and failure also limit the impact of QI. Dixon-Woods and Martin (2016) propose four ways to improve the quality of QI efforts. The first relates to the need to take a whole systems approach or what the authors term as a sector-like entity approach by, for instance, agreeing standard operating procedures. The second is the need to stop looking for 'magic bullets' and focus on the structures to support improvement and learn from examples of exceptional good performance. The third is the need to build capacity for designing and testing solutions and an ability to build high-quality prototypes that can be modelled and tested prior to full implementation. The fourth way is the need to plan for long-term programmes of work which are resourced appropriately to support the learning, evidence and dissemination of QI.

The desire to limit healthcare improvement to tools and techniques has been one of the main criticisms of QI endeavours. We have seen a considerable growth in the use of process mapping, checklists, trigger tools, run charts and driver diagrams which have produced some effective change. However, to isolate training and education to these areas without considering the environmental and social context within which healthcare is delivered may be limiting ambition and desire for whole system and sustainable change. Like other scholars (e.g. Batalden and Davidoff 2007) Lucas (2015) argues that healthcare services are unlikely to realise their full potential until improvement is recognised as being part of every worker's job. For this to occur he advocates a shift in the way that people learn about improvement and the need for them to unlearn practices that may well inhibit their ability to learn new ways of working. Lucas (2015) believes at an individual level there is a need for considerable habit change which will then permeate the teams and social interactions within our workplaces.

Usefully Lucas (2015) suggests quality improvers require five core habits (and actions) these being learning, influencing, resilience, creativity and systems thinking. In order to develop such habits, it will be necessary to reframe the way in which QI is taught. Before then, he advocates that we need to further understand the habits of reliable action, particularly of those who are able to cultivate sustainable improvement. Although we will not examine these habits within this research, it is important to include this contemporary work here as one of the ambitions of this publication is to move forward the discussions and research agenda within this emerging discipline.

Conclusions

This chapter has considered three disciplines that overlap but also bring a different perspective in which to examine the (re)design of patient pathways (see Fig. 1.2). Quality improvement and systems thinking are probably more prominent in healthcare than SCM, but we see all three lenses will assist in identifying the enablers and inhibitors to achieving integrated healthcare delivery systems and will bring some insight to the use of lean, agile and leagility in pathway design. Encouraging healthcare managers and professionals to think in terms of whole systems will help to develop the scientific mind advocated by Peters (2014). Similarly, highlighting the work of Lucas (2015) will also help those involved and those yet to be engaged in improving healthcare to think about the skills, habits and minds required by individuals to support operationalising some of the recommendations proposed by this study.

Before moving to take a closer look at the key concepts which have shaped this study (lean, agile and leagility), it is appropriate here to reflect on the terminology used. Systems thinking, SCM and QI originate from industrial settings. It could be argued that systems thinking and QI have developed some traction within healthcare. There is less theoretical evidence of SCM in healthcare, particularly outside of "factory-like" settings (e.g. supply of medicines). Although we will continue to use the term "SCM" in this study, there may be some value in considering other terminology which is more accessible to those involved in delivery of healthcare, for example, care chain management. We suggest this with some caution as chain may well suggest a linear approach which may not reflect the design of the pathways we study here.

References

Aronsson, H., Abrahamsson, M., & Spens, K. (2011). Developing lean and agile health care supply chains. *Supply Chain Management*, 16(3), 176–183.

Batalden, P., & Davidoff, F. (2007). What is "quality improvement" and how can it transform healthcare?. *BMJ Quality & Safety*, 16, 2–3.

Berwick, D. (1989). Continuous improvement as an ideal in health care. *New England Journal of Medicine, 320,* 53–56.
Bicheno, J. (2008). *The lean toolbox for service systems.* Buckingham: PICSIE books.
Blumenthal, D., & Kilo, C. (1998). A report card on continuous quality improvement. *The Millbank Quarterly, 76*(4), 625–648.
Böhme, T., Williams, S. J., Childerhouse, P., Deakin, E., & Towill, D. (2013). Methodology challenges associated with benchmarking healthcare supply chains. *Production Planning & Control, 24*(10–11), 1002–1014.
Böhme, T., Williams, S. J., Childerhouse, P., Deakin, E., & Towill, D. (2014). Squaring the circle of healthcare supplies. *Journal of Health, Organisation and Management, 28*(2), 247–265.
Braithwaite, J., Iedema, R. A., & Jorm, C. (2007). Trust, communication, theory of mind and social brain hypothesis: Deep explanations for what goes wrong in health care. *Journal of Health Organisation and Management, 21*(4/5), 353–367.
Brennan, S., McKenzie, J., Whitty, P., Buchan, H., & Green, S. (2009), Continuous quality improvement: Effects on professional practice and healthcare outcomes, *Cochrane Database of Systematic Reviews.* doi: 10.1002/14651858.CD003319.pub2.
Burgess, N., & Radnor, Z. (2013). Evaluating lean in healthcare. *International Journal of Health Care Quality Assurance, 26*(3), 220–235.
Byrnes, J. (2004), Fixing the healthcare supply chain, Boston, MA: Working Knowledge, Harvard Business School. Available at: http://hbswk.hbs.edu/archive/4036html [Accessed July 20, 2016].
Campbell, D. P. (1958). *Process dynamics.* New York: McGraw-Hill.
Checkland, P. (1999). Systems Thinking, in Currie, W. and Galliers, B.A. *Rethinking Management Information Systems: An interdisciplinary perspective,* OUP, Oxford.
Childerhouse, P., & Towill, D. R. (2002). Analysis of the factors affecting real-world value stream performance. *International Journal of Production Research, 40*(15), 3499–3518.
Christopher, M. (1992). *Logistics and supply chain management.* London: Pitman Publishing.
De Vries, J., & Huijsman, R. (2011). Supply chain management in health services: An overview. *Supply Chain Management: An International Journal, 16*(3), 159–165.
Dixon-Woods, M., & Martin, G. (2016). Does quality improvement improve quality? *Future Hospital Journal,* 3(3), 191–194.
Elmaghraby, S. E. (1966). *The design of production systems.* New York: Reinhold.
Glenday, I. (2005). Moving to flow (levelled production). *Manufacturing Engineer, 84*(2), 20–23.
Grol, R., Wensing, M., Bosch, M., Hulscher, M., & Eccles, M. (2013). Theories on implementation of change in healthcare. In R. Grol, M. Wensing, M. Eccles, &

D. Davis (Eds.), *Improving patient care: The implementation of change in health care* (2nd edition). Chichester, West Sussex: John Wiley & Sons.

Jessup, M., Wallis, M., Boyle, J., Crilly, J., Lind, J., Green, D., Fitzgerald, G. (2010). Implementing an emergency department patient admission predictive tool: Insights from practice. *Journal of Health Organization and Management*, 24(3), 306–318.

Karvonen, S., Ra Mo, J., Leijala, M., & Holmstrom, J. (2004). Productivity improvement in heart surgery – a case study on care process development. *Production Planning and Control*, 15(3), 238–246.

Kelle, P., Schneider, H., Wiley-Patton, S., & Woosley, J. (2009). Healthcare supply chain management. In M. Jaber (Ed.). *Inventory management: Nonclassical views*. Boco Raton, FL: CRC Press.

Lambert, D., James, M., Stock, R., & Ellram, L. (1998). *Fundamentals of logistics management*. Boston, MA: Irwin/McGraw-Hill.

Lee, S. M., Lee, D. H., & Schniederjans, M. J. (2011). Supply chain innovation and organisational performance in the healthcare industry. *International Journal of Operations and Production Management*, 31(11), 1193–1214.

Lucas, B. (2015). Getting the improvement habit. *BMJ Quality & Safety*, Published Online First: [30th December 2015]. doi:10.1136/bmjqs-2015-005086.

Mason-Jones, R., & Towill, D. R. (1998). Shrinking the supply chain uncertainty circle. *Control, The Institute of Operations Management*, 24(7), 17–22.

McKone-Sweet, K. E., Hamilton, P., & Willis, S. B. (2005). The ailing healthcare supply chain: A prescription for change. *Journal of Supply Chain Management*, 41(1), 4–17.

Meijboom, B., Schmidt-Bakx, S., & Westert, G. (2011). Supply chain management practices for improving patient-oriented care. *Supply Chain Management: An International Journal*, 16(3), 166–175.

Mustaffa, N. H., & Potter, A. (2009). Healthcare supply chain management in Malaysia: A case study. *Supply Chain Management: An International Journal*, 14(3), 234–243.

Ohno, T. (1988). *Toyota production systems: Beyond large scale production*. Cambridge, MA: Productivity Press.

Parnaby, J., & Towill, D. R. (2008). Seamless healthcare delivery systems. *International Journal of Health Care Quality Assurance*, 21(3), 249–273.

Peters, D. (2014). The application of systems thinking in health: Why use systems thinking?. *Health Research Policy and Systems*, 12(51), 2014, 1–6.

Schmenner, R. W., & Swink, M. L. (1998). Theory in operations management. *Journal of Operations Management*, 17, 97–113.

Schneller, E., & Smeltzer, L. (2006). *Strategic management of the health care supply chain*. San Francisco, CA: Jossey-Bass.

Shah, R., Goldstein, S. M., Unger, B. T., & Henry, T. D. (2008). Explaining anomalous high performance in a health care supply chain. *Decision Sciences*, *29*(4), 759–789.

Shih, S., Rivers, P., & Sonya Hus, H. (2009). Strategic information technology alliances for effective health-care supply chain management. *Health Care Management Research*, *22*(3), 140–150.

Shortell, S., Bennett, C., & Byrk, G. (1998). Assessing the impact of Continuous Quality Improvement on clinical practice: What it will take to accelerate progress. *Milbank Quarterly*, *76*, 593–624.

Spear, S. (2005). Fixing healthcare from the inside. *Today, Harvard Business Review*, *83*(9), 78–91.

Sterman, J. (2001). System dynamics modelling: Tools for learning in a complex world. *California Management Review*, *43*(4), 8–25.

Towill, D. R. (1997). The seamless supply chain—the predator's strategic advantage. *International Journal of Technology Management*, *13*(1), 37–56.

Walley, P., Silvester, K., Steyn, R., & Conway, J. B. (2006). Managing variation in demand: Lessons from the UK National Health Service. *Journal of Healthcare Management*, *51*(5), 309–322.

Walley, P. (2013). Does the public sector need a more demand-driven approach to capacity management?. *Production Planning & Control*, *24*(10–11), 877–890.

Werr, A., Stjernberg, T., & Docherty, P. (1997). The functions of methods of change in management consultancy. *Journal of Organisational and Management Change*, *10*(4), 288–307.

Young, T., Brailsford, S., Connell, C., Davies, R., Harper, P., & Klein, J. (2004). Using industrial processes to improve patient care. *British Medical Journal*, *328*, 162–164.

CHAPTER 3

Lean in Healthcare

Abstract This chapter provides a synthesis of the growing literature associated with the employment of the popular approach to improvement and supply chain design—lean thinking. It also endeavours to capture the breadth and depth of lean implementation in healthcare both in terms of an approach to improvement and the design of supply chains. Briefly the origins of lean are discussed followed by the applications within healthcare. This synthesis of the literature identifies five key themes: prominence of lean in secondary care, role of standardisation, focus on tools, sustainability, and dealing with professional and functional silos. The critics of lean are included along with some of the contemporary areas of research associated with improving patient satisfaction, readiness and effectiveness of lean in healthcare.

Keywords Lean · Supply chain · Quality improvement · Healthcare

INTRODUCTION

This chapter provides a synthesis of the growing literature associated with the employment of the popular approach to improvement and supply chain design—lean thinking. It is outside the scope of this chapter to provide a systematic review of the literature but it refers to the review papers which have synthesised the growing number of publications in this area. Often quality improvement and redesign of healthcare services

© The Author(s) 2017
S.J. Williams, *Improving Healthcare Operations*,
DOI 10.1007/978-3-319-46913-3_3

employ approaches other than lean (e.g. Six Sigma) which are out of the scope of this study. Similarly, lean principles might be used by healthcare organisations but the approach may not be referred to as lean. Therefore, it is difficult to fully estimate how much lean has penetrated the redesigning and improving of healthcare services. This chapter endeavours to capture the breadth and depth of lean implementation in healthcare both in terms of an approach to improvement and the design of supply chains.

Fundamentals of Lean Thinking

The term "lean" originates from a study of the Toyota Production System (TPS) and was popularised by the bestseller book *The Machine That Changed the World* (Womack et al. 1990). Twenty-five years on Samuel et al. (2015) evaluate the impact of this text. The authors identify four key themes: lean as a representation of TPS which highlighted the origins and antecedents of lean; lean as a process improvement methodology which highlighted the need to compare lean with other process improvement methodologies; lean as a movement which highlighted the characteristics of lean's evolution over time; and lean as academic body of literature which highlighted the diversity of perspective and opinion that lean has inspired.

Since 2001 in the UK and 2002 in the USA (Radnor and Osborne 2013) lean thinking is established as one of the improvement methodologies that has become a prominent and popular approach in reforming healthcare services. This popularity is confirmed by the publication of over 90 academic writings in ten different countries since its inception in 2001 (Brandao De Souza 2009). This growth in interest is associated with the "double focus of Lean on customer satisfaction and employee involvement which suits the culture of most care centres". Other similarities between lean and healthcare are the focus on customers, quality, safety and staff (Bohmer and Ferlins 2006, p. 4).

A recent literature review conducted by Costa and Filho (2016) reports how lean continues to be popular in healthcare and lists its implementation in areas such as theatres, emergency departments, mental health centres, pharmacy, outpatients, ophthalmology, radiology, audiology and cardiology. They also identify 24 lean tools being used which include mapping, 5S (workplace organisation), PDSA cycles and standardised work. In addition to the approach some studies note the positive measurable outcomes of lean initiatives, for example, LaGanga's (2011) study of an outpatients service in the USA demonstrated how a lean project increased the throughput of patients by 27% and reduced the 'did not attend' rate by 12% (for other examples see Graban and Swatz 2012 and Toussaint and Berry 2013).

A number of frameworks (e.g. house of lean) have also been proposed for implementing lean in public services and healthcare (e.g. Radnor 2010; Ogden and Moncy nd). Common components include workplace organisation (5S), visual management, system or process view, stable and standardised processes, understanding customer value/expectations, managing demand and capacity and structured problem solving.

Shah and Ward (2007) and Samuel et al. (2015) report that, despite the fact that there is a plethora of academic and practitioner writings, there is still no confirmed definition of lean. Womack and Jones (1996) helpfully provide five lean principles as a framework for organisations to use to implement lean thinking. The first principle focuses on understanding value from the perspective of the customer. The second involves defining the value streams or processes that will add and deliver value to the customer. The third involves making the processes flow without any delays or interruptions. The fourth emphasises the need for products or services to be pulled at the demand or need of the customer. The final principle is concerned with continuous improvement and the need for organisations to strive for perfection. These principles are often adapted for healthcare by combining principles three and four and including an additional principle which focuses on the empowerment of staff. Alternatively, Toussaint and Gerard (2010) translate these principles for healthcare as: (1) focus on the patient; (2) design care around the patient; (3) identifying value for the patient; (4) removing everything else (waste); and (5) reducing time to treatment and for the remainder of the journey. Radnor et al. (2012) emphasise the key assumptions of lean (see Table 3.1) and suggest that without these lean is likely to fail.

Table 3.1 Key assumptions of lean thinking

Defining value and waste from the perspective of the customer (patient) or end-user
Creating value by either reducing non-value-adding activities or increasing value-adding activities at no extra cost
Appreciating there is defined and measurable benefits to the organisation
Freeing up resources that can help to continue to improve processes
Understanding the "heart" of lean is the concept of customer value
Ensuring the main focus remains on quality and safety rather than on cost

---
Adapted from Radnor et al. (2012)

Womack and Jones (1996) recognised that only a small fraction of the total time and effort taken to produce a product or deliver a service actually added value for the end customer. Hence the need to clearly define value for a specific product or service from the end customer's perspective and to ensure that all non-value activities—or waste—are removed. Waste can be defined as any part of a process that adds time, effort or cost but no value. Originally Ohno (1988) classified these non-value activities into seven categories. Guimarâes and Carvalho (2013) provide healthcare examples of waste:

- over-production of diagnostic tests,
- transportation (patients, equipment, etc.),
- inventory (clinical and non-clinical supplies) and work in progress (tests waiting distribution),
- over-processing (excessive documentation or duplication of documentation),
- waiting (patients being patient),
- correction/defects (prescription errors, incorrect information, incorrect diagnosis) and
- motion (looking for missing patient information, sharing medical equipment/tools).

From their analysis of the annual reports from English NHS Trusts, Burgess and Radnor (2013) provided a typology for different levels of implementation of lean within the trusts (see Table 3.2). Across two time

Table 3.2 Typology of lean implementation in England NHS hospitals

Tentative	Considering lean and possibly piloting small projects or seeking external assistance
Productive Ward only	Implementing Productive Ward or Productive Theatre (the former NHS Institute of Innovation and Improvement initiative) but no other evidence of lean
Few projects	Evidence of lean principles being used to underpin improvement projects across different parts of the organisation
Programme	Lean principles being used to underpin 1- to 5-year programmes
Systemic	Reference made to embedding lean in the organisation as a whole, recognised training programme for lean and adopting a local approach to how lean can be implemented

Adapted from Burgess and Radnor (2013)

points the study found that the majority of hospitals were implementing Productive Ward or had initiated a few lean projects. Few organisations were operating at a systemic level.

Lean from a Supply Chain Perspective

Early definitions of lean supply (e.g. Lamming 1996) were premised on the entire supply chain from raw materials to the end consumer, where organisational boundaries and interfaces were seen as artificial with the aim of creating value for the consumer at all stages within the supply chain. The implication for suppliers was to become closely integrated with their customers in four key processes: quality, delivery, cost and design. These suppliers needed to then cascade these new working practices to their suppliers and others further down the supply chain (Hines 1994). More recently, Martínez-Jurado and Moyano-Fuentes (2014), from a review of the literature, confirmed the defining characteristics of lean supply chain management to be:

- long-term collaborative relationships based on mutual trust,
- small number of suppliers achieved through single or dual supply,
- good levels of communication and information sharing,
- early involvement of suppliers in new product design/development,
- strict quality processes and measurement systems and
- frequent feedback, shared risk and benefits and working together to achieve best outcome for all parties.

Given this study is focusing on pathway design it is important to consider lean within the context of the supply chain. Although most of the research in this area has been considered within manufacturing and the flow of materials, it is anticipated some of the above characteristics are appropriate to the flow of patients and the ability to deliver seamless healthcare.

Critics of Lean

Despite the popularity of lean, some authors believe lean implementation to be pragmatic, patchy and fragmented (e.g. Proudlove et al. 2008; Young and McClean 2008). Burgess and Radnor's (2013) recent evaluation of lean in English NHS Trust found implementation tended to be isolated rather than system-wide but overtime the use of lean is increasing and progressing more to Trusts' adopting a systemic approach. Similarly, Joosten et al. (2009) report how the emphasis, particularly for lean in healthcare, has been process-oriented and little attention has been paid to the socio-technical aspects and "respect-for-humans-system".

Some writers are sceptical as to whether improvement approaches such as lean can help to deliver person-centred care. For example, Kelly quotes the work of Parker and Slaughter (1988) where lean is described as "management by stress". He refers to lean in healthcare being driven by a relentless need for improvement which is delivered by fewer and fewer staff, which can ultimately result in burnout. He goes on to say that healthcare staff have to try and reconcile the need to deliver high-quality care with corporate (and possibly national) efficiency targets often associated with the introduction of lean improvement programmes. Similarly, Seddon (2010) warns of the human cost which can manifest itself in chronic low morale. Kelly (2013) warns the austerity pressures within the global economy are likely to encourage more organisations to pursue lean as a way of gaining efficiencies rather than improving the quality of care.

It is the focus on efficiency alone that is at odds with the improvement agenda. Waring and Bishop (2010) note managers' tendency to focus on efficiency and productivity over quality and patient experience. Lean was originally introduced as an approach to quality improvement. It can provide cost savings but should not do so at the expense of safety and quality. Of course, in times of austerity the urgency in which to demonstrate these savings is much greater. The need to view lean (and other approaches to improvement) as a philosophy, a way of doing things, must not be lost. There is a need to build improvement capability and capacity within organisations; this means that freed-up time and resource is reinvested in improvement and that this does not result in removing people from the organisation. Womack and Jones (1996) were very clear in their writings around lean, in that it should not be used as a mechanism for downsizing and any reduction in staff should take place before lean is implemented. They recognised that most organisations would need to build their capability in the use of improvement tools, and as non-value-adding activities are removed and processes redesigned, then the resources are reinvested in future improvement programmes.

Key Themes in the Lean Healthcare Literature

A synthesis of academic writings on lean in healthcare can be divided into five key themes:

1. Secondary care (hospital) setting: The majority of papers reviewed refer to research that has been conducted in the acute (hospital) setting (e.g. Coffin 2013; Vats et al. 2012). The most popular areas include the emergency department (e.g. Dickson et al. 2009), surgery (e.g. Mandahawi et al. 2011) and the ward (e.g. Morrow et al. 2012). Few papers consider the patient journey beyond the initial care setting in which the research is undertaken. The need to extend the research across organisational boundaries is a challenging but necessary call for future research.
2. Role of standardisation: Standardisation is an area of lean that has generated some debate in terms of whether it is appropriate for healthcare. Many healthcare professionals believe that standardisation and the delivery of healthcare are at odds, particularly as the needs of patients can be complex and therefore the care they need will vary considerably. However, it is important to make the distinction between standardisation of care and the standardisation of processes employed to deliver healthcare services. Understanding variability and variation is fundamental to the redesign of patient pathways and healthcare services generally.
3. Tool focus rather than patient focus: Many of the studies (e.g. Radnor et al. 2012) describe the tools and techniques that have been employed within improvement programmes. Although it is important for the development of theory to understand how these are being adopted for use in healthcare, there is also a need to report the benefits to patients. Much of the commentary focuses on how these tools and techniques have been implemented and there is less evidence on what difference these have made in relation to improvement of services for patients and staff and the wider healthcare system.
4. Sustainability is an issue that some papers allude to in relation to lean in healthcare. Specifically, Radnor et al. (2012) from their case analysis of four UK hospitals report lean to be on the "fringes" of service transformation. Whilst the organisations reported short-term gains the majority failed to deliver more widespread and sustained

improvements. The main reason given for these sustainability problems was the tool-based implementation. A more recent case (Burgess et al. 2015) reports on the demise of a whole systems approach to improvement as a result of a financial and performance crisis.

5. Professional and functional silos: One of the main barriers to lean healthcare is reported to stem from how healthcare organisations are structured and the fragmentation of care and professional practice (Brandão de Souza and Pidd 2011). A professional silo refers to the professional groupings, of which a typical hospital might have a hundred or more. A simple professional division can be made between medical (e.g. doctors, nurses, therapists etc.) and non-medical (managers, administrators, finance, HR, etc.) staff. Some professional silos can be further divided into sub-silos which also include distinctions for seniority (e.g. registrars, junior doctors). This complex structure of professional silos is likely to inhibit or compromise communication and levels of interaction (Brandão de Souza and Pidd 2011).

A functional silo may contain members of many different professional silos (e.g. surgery may include general surgery, orthopaedics, anaesthetists, etc.) or those departments that undertake specific tasks such as phlebotomy, imaging, pharmacy, etc. Functional silos often lead to care being fragmented with the performance of single silos being improved but overall patient care being diminished (Mann 2005).

Contemporary Writings on Lean in Healthcare

Some of the more contemporary areas and issues emerging from the literature are summarised below.

Improved Patient Satisfaction

Some advocates of lean propose it helps to improve patient satisfaction in several ways: it helps to pursue the "perfect patient experience" (Kenney 2010), increases value (Wellman et al. 2010) and improves quality and safety of care (Graban 2008). However, Poksinska et al. (2016) propose there is no clear evidence to link implementing lean with improved levels of patient satisfaction. From a mixed-method investigation of patient satisfaction surveys and primary care case analysis they conclude lean healthcare implementation primarily targets efficiency and little attention is paid to the patient's perspective. This is interesting given that the first principle of lean is understanding value from the viewpoint of the consumer. It is unclear whether this "consumer" focus has been lost in translation from the manufacturing form of lean or the lack of clarity in relation to who occupies the jurisdiction of being the "consumer". There is much discussion of healthcare being viewed from a multi-stakeholder perspective and often this is lack of clarity in terms of who is the customer (internal) and who is the consumer. When viewing a patient pathway it might be concluded there are internal customers (e.g. next part of the process - A&E to ward) and external customers (e.g. GP referal to Outpatient clinic) customers and then the consumer of the care which is the patient. Within the literature there does not appear to be any consensus in relation to the narrative customer or consumer. The proposal put forward here in relation to internal and external customer does lend itself to a supply chain context.

DiGioia et al. (2015) report on the interest expressed by healthcare organisations that have invested time and resources in the Patient and Family Centered Care Methodology and Practice (PFCC M/P). They propose that interest is fuelled by the need to address the challenge of keeping the patient (and family) as the primary focus of improvement activities and to add patient experience as an equal focus with eliminating waste. They note the difficulties some healthcare organisations have in maintaining the patient focus required to support lean implementation and suggest the combination of lean and PFCC M/P can accelerate the pace of improvement. The additional features of the PFCC M/P are reported to be:

- voice of patient to include family members,
- shadowing of patients and family members to identify all touch points within the patient journey,
- heightening staff autonomy, engagement and empowerment and
- integrating lean with PFCC M/P bridges "top-down" and "bottom-up" approaches to change and helps to move from transactional to transformational change.

One of the key recommendations from DiGioia et al. (2015) is the need for the shadowing of the process. Again this is an interesting observation. If we refer to the original forms of lean, it advocated the need to "walk the process" or "go to the gemba". It is possible that the authors here are suggesting a more detailed observation of the patient journey but it is unclear whether the integration of these approaches will provide any value, except the reinforcement of the patient-centredness required for healthcare improvement and redesign efforts.

Readiness for Lean Implementation

As noted earlier in this chapter, the focus of lean has long been reported to be on tools and techniques and "how to" (see e.g. Graban 2008, 2011) rather than the contextual and philosophical elements of the concept. Recently there has been a call for a shift of emphasis to readiness and preparation of the foundations for implementing lean. The ability to assess whether individuals, teams and organisations are ready for large-scale change is often overlooked and not given sufficient attention.

Other interesting work which we can relate to readiness and preparation for change is the use of the Plan-Do-Study-Act (PDSA) cycle which has become extremely popular in healthcare. The PDSA cycle is central to Nolan's model for improvement (a three-stage approach defining the aims, measures, ideas) and is also known as the Deming or Shewart cycle. The PDSA cycle is centred on the concept of iterative tests of change. Some scholars have raised concerns over its application and the complexity of its use in practice (Walley and Gowland 2004; Taylor et al. 2014; Reed and Card 2016). Some question whether the approach is appropriate to address the significant challenges of healthcare improvement (Dixon-Woods et al. 2014).

The review by Reed and Card (2016) identifies several shortcomings of how the PDSA cycle has been used in healthcare. The misjudgement of the resources and support, which includes inadequate human resources and financial support, results in many projects failing. Often the projects produce no real improvements and yet the prevailing healthcare culture of "just get on with it" and "do, do, do" is difficult to overcome. The authors propose in order to be successful the use of PDSA must be supported by a significant investment in leadership, expertise and resources for change, all factors associated with readiness for change. The ability and discipline to ensure that the "plan" element of the cycle is not overlooked or rushed is critical to the success of using the PDSA cycle but also the opportunity to learn from both successes and failures. The courage and ability to halt a failing project was also seen as a key decision that was often misplaced in healthcare.

Another popular tool that has emerged in healthcare improvement is the use of A3 reporting. This is a tool that originated from the TPS and has been embraced by some organisations, but its use has been sporadic. Advocates (e.g. Jimmerson 2007) saw the real potential for this planning and reporting tool to be central to improvement projects. However, it would seem that the value of this mechanism has not been sustained or fully embedded into the reporting functions within healthcare systems. Hence the application of this useful tool has not stood the test of time particularly in the UK. It is likely that in other countries such as the US and Australia the use of A3 is much more prevalent.

Effectiveness of Lean Interventions in Healthcare

As noted earlier, quality improvement is central to the discussion on healthcare reform, yet the means of achieving it remain complex and not well understood. The success rate of improvement programmes is somewhat variable across similar settings and early successes are often difficult to replicate (Lomas 2005; Dixon-Woods et al. 2011). The ability to link improvement activities with outcomes is fundamental to understanding why and how interventions work. Similarly, the interaction between the context and the programme is also important (Øvretveit 2011; Harvey et al. 2011).

A recent systematic review of the literature examining those lean interventions in healthcare that included quantitative data has been conducted (Moraros et al. 2016). This review identified 22 articles of which 4 were concerned with health outcomes, 3 included both health and process outcomes and 15 included only process outcomes. The authors made three key findings; first there was no statistically significant association with patient satisfaction and health outcomes; second there was a negative association with financial costs and worker satisfaction; and third potential, and yet inconsistent, benefits on process outcomes like patient flow and safety. They suggest that there is no evidence that lean interventions lead to quality improvements in healthcare, with a call for more rigorous and high-quality scientific research to be conducted that will ascertain impact and effectiveness of lean in healthcare settings.

Critics continue to voice their scepticism of importing improvement techniques that have originated from other industries. The context of improvement work has become more of a focus as quality improvement matures as a discipline and approach within healthcare. The complexities and nuances of the various healthcare settings are fundamental to understanding what improvement approaches to use and when. However, according to Stame (2004) much of the operational elements of improvement activities remain as a "black box". To date, a key focus for improvement has been on implementation and less on the architecture of pathways and supporting structures. This study contributes to the call to widen the scope of improvement in healthcare by examining the design of two care pathways which extend across both primary and secondary care.

Conclusions

Lean thinking has become a popular approach to improvement in healthcare. The challenge for healthcare, as with other sectors, is to reduce the temptation to solely focus on tools and pay limited attention to the organisational context and readiness to support the desired change. The pragmatism that is seen in medicine and generally in healthcare needs to be channelled to ensure sufficient effort is put into the planning of improvement activities, which includes ensuring appropriate process and outcome measures are in place.

Lean thinking definitely has an important role to play in improving our healthcare services. It is not, however, a "one size fits all" scenario and healthcare improvers need to become skilled at knowing which improvement method, approach, tool to use and when. Lean focuses on removing waste, creating value, improving flow and standardising processes where possible. Some healthcare professionals refute lean by calling for a greater degree of flexibility in the system and a move away from standardisation which they believe may limit their skills. In the next chapter we consider agility, an approach which has been widely used in the design of manufacturing supply chains and consider what role it has to play in the design of healthcare services.

References

Bohmer, R., & Ferlins, E. M. (2006). Virginia Mason Medical Center, Harvard Business School Case 606-044, Harvard Business School, Boston, MA.

Brandão De Souza, L. (2009). Trends and approaches in lean healthcare. *Leadership in Health Services*, 22(2), 121–139.

Brandão de Souza, L., & Pidd, M. (2011). Exploring the barriers to lean health care implementation. *Public Money & Management*, 31(1), 59–66.

Burgess, N., & Radnor, Z. (2013). Evaluating lean in healthcare. *International Journal of Health Care Quality Assurance*, 26(3), 220–235.

Burgess, N., Radnor, Z., & Furnival, J. (2015). Delivery not departments: A case study of a whole organisation approach to lean implementation across an English hospital. In Z. Radnor, N. Bateman, A. Esain, M. Kumar, S. Williams, & D. Upton (Eds.), *Public service operations management* (pp. 310–327). Abingdon, Oxon: Routledge.

Coffin, C. T. (2013). The continuous improvement process and ergonomics in ultrasound department. *Radiology Management*, 35(1), 22–25.

Costa, L. B. M., & Filho, M. G. (2016). Lean healthcare: Review. *Classification and Analysis of Literature, Production Planning & Control*, 27(10), 826–836.

Dickson, E., Singh, S., Cheung, D., Wyatt, C., & Nugent, A. (2009). Application of lean manufacturing techniques in the Emergency Department. *Journal of Emergency Medicine*, 37(2), 177–182.

DiGioia, A., Greenhouse, P., Chermak, T., & Hayden, M. (2015). A case for integrating the patient and family centred care methodology and practice in Lean healthcare organisations. *Healthcare*, 3, 225–230.

Dixon-Woods, M., Bosk, C., Aveling, E., Goeschel, C., & Pronovost, P. (2011). Explaining Michigan: Developing an ex post theory of a quality improvement program. *Milbank Quarterly*, 89(2), 67–205.

Dixon-Woods, M., Martin, G., Tarrant, C., Bion, J., Goeschel, C., Pronovost, P., Woodcock, T. (2014). Safer clinical systems: Evaluation findings. London: Health Foundation. http://www.health.org.uk/sites/default/files/ [Accessed 23rd June 2016].

Graban, M. (2008). *Lean hospitals: Improving quality, patient safety and employee satisfaction*. Boca Raton, FL: Productivity Press.

Graban, M. (2011). *Lean hospitals: Improving quality, patient safety and employee engagement* (2nd edition). Boca Raton, FL: CRC Press.

Graban, M., & Swartz, J. (2012). Change for health. *Management Services*, 56(2), 35–39.

Guimarâes, C., & Carvalho, J. (2013). Strategic outsourcing: A lean tool of healthcare supply chain management. *Strategic Outsourcing: An International Journal*, 6(2), 138–166.

Harvey, G., Fitzgerald, L., Fielden, S., McBride, A., Waterman, H., Bamford, D., Boaden, R. (2011). The NIHR collaboration for leadership in applied health research and care (CLAHRC) for greater Manchester: Combining empirical. *Theoretical and Experiential Evidence to Design and Evaluate a Large-Scale Implementation Strategy, Implementation Science*, 6(1), 96–107.

Hines, P. (1994). *Creating world-class suppliers: Unlocking mutual competitive advantage*. London: Pitman publishing Ltd.

Jimmerson, C. (2007). *A3 Problem solving for healthcare: A practical method for eliminating waste.* New York: HCP Press.

Joosten, T., Bongers, I., & Janssen, R. (2009). Application of lean thinking to healthcare: Issues and observations. *International Journal for Quality in Health Care, 21*(5), 341–347.

Kelly, J. (2013). The effect of lean systems on person-centred care. *Nursing Times, 109*(13), 16–17.

Kenney, C. (2010). *Transforming health care: Virginia Mason Medical Center's pursuit of the perfect patient experience.* New York: Productivity Press.

LaGanga, L. (2011). Lean service operations: Reflections and new directions for capacity expansion in outpatient clinics. *Journal of Operations Management, 29*(5), 422–433.

Lamming, R. (1996). Squaring lean supply with supply chain management. *International Journal of Operations & Production Management, 16*(2), 196–183.

Lomas, J. (2005). Using research to inform healthcare managers' and policy-makers' questions: From summative to interpretive synthesis. *Healthcare Policy, 1*(1), 55–71.

Mandahawi, N., Al-Araidah, O., Boran, A., & Khasawneh, M. (2011). Application of Lean Six Sigma tools to minimise length of stay for ophthalmology day case surgery. *International Journal of Six Sigma and Competitive Advantage, 6*(3), 156–172.

Mann, L. (2005). From 'silos' to seamless health care: Bringing hospitals and GPs back together again. *Medical Journal of Australia, 182,* 34–37.

Martínez-Jurado, P., & Moyano-Fuentes, J. (2014). Lean management, supply chain management and sustainability. *A Literature Review, Journal of Cleaner Production, 85,* 134–150.

Moraros, J., Lemstra, M., & Nwankwo, C. (2016). Lean interventions in healthcare: Do they actually work? A systematic literature review. *International Journal for Quality in Health Care, 28*(2), 150–165.

Morrow, E., Robert, G., Maben, J., & Griffiths, P. (2012). Implementing large-scale quality improvement: Lessons from The Productive Ward: Releasing Time to Care™. *International Journal of Health Care Quality Assurance, 25*(4), 237–253.

Ogden, G., & Moncy, B. (nd), Lean Healthcare: Creating a Lean-thinking culture, GE Healthcare, Available at http://partners.gehealthcare.com/WP-Creating%20LTC%20HR_15May09.pdf [Accessed June 8, 2016].

Ohno, T. (1988). *Toyota production system; Beyond large scale production.* Portland, OR: Productivity Press.

Øvretveit, J. (2011). Understanding the conditions for improvement: Research to discover which context influences affect improvement success. *British Medical Journal Quality and Safety, 20,* i18–i23.

Parker, M., & Slaughter, J. (1988). *Choosing sides: Unions and the team concept*. Boston, MA: South End Press.
Poksinska, B., Fialkowska-Filipek, M., & Engstrom, J. (2016, published online first 10 February 2016). Does Lean healthcare improve patient satisfaction? A mixed-method investigation into primary care. *BMJ Quality & Safety*.
Proudlove, N., Moxham, C., & Boaden, R. (2008). Lessons for lean in healthcare from using Six Sigma in the NHS. *Public Money & Management*, 28(1), 27–34.
Radnor, Z. (2010). *Review of business process improvement methodologies in public services*. London: Advanced Institute of Management Research report.
Radnor, Z., Holweg, M., & Waring, J. (2012). Lean in healthcare: The unfilled promise?. *Social Science & Medicine*, 74(3), 364–371.
Radnor, Z., & Osborne, S. (2013). Lean: A failed theory for public services?. *Public Management Review*, 15(2), 265–287.
Reed, J., & Card, A. (2016). The problem with Plan-Do-Study-Act Cycles. *BMJ Quality and Safety*, 25(3), 147–152.
Samuel, D., Found, P., & Williams, S. (2015). How did the publication of the book The Machine That Changed The World change management thinking? Exploring 25 years of lean literature. *International Journal of Operations & Production Management*, 35(10), 1386–1407.
Seddon, J. (2010), How Lean became mean, Vanguard Consulting. Available at www.tinurl.com/vanguard-lean [Accessed June 15, 2016].
Shah, R., & Ward, P. (2007). Defining and developing measures of lean production. *Journal of Operations Management*, 25(4), 785–805.
Stame, N. (2004). Theory-based evaluation and types of complexity. *Evaluation*, 10(1), 58.
Taylor, M. J., McNicholas, C., Nicolay, C., Darzi, A., Bell, D., & Reed, J. (2014). Systematic review of the application of the plan-do-study-act method to improve quality in healthcare. *BMJ Quality and Safety*, 23, 290–298.
Toussaint, J., & Berry, L. (2013). The promise of lean in health care. *Mayo Clinic Proceedings*, 88(1), 74–82.
Toussaint, J., & Gerard, R. (2010). *On the mend*. Cambridge, MA: Lean Enterprise Institute.
Vats, A., Goin, K., Villarreal, M., Vilmaz, T., Fortenberry, J., & Keskinocak, P. (2012). The impact of lean rounding process in a paediatric intensive care unit. *Critical Care Medicine*, 40(2), 607–617.
Walley, P., & Gowland, B. (2004). Completing the circle: From P-D to PDSA. *International Journal of Health Care Quality Assurance*, 17(6), 349-58.
Waring, J., & Bishop, S. (2010). Lean healthcare: rhetoric, ritual and resistance. *Social Science & Medicine*, 71(7), 1332–1340.
Wellman, J., Jeffries, H., & Hagan, P. (2010). *Leading the lean healthcare journey: Driving culture change to increase value*. New York: Productivity Press.

Womack, J., & Jones, D. (1996). *Lean thinking: Banish waste and create wealth in your corporation.* New York: Simon Schuster.

Womack, J., Jones, D., & Roos, D. (1990). *The machine that changed the world.* New York: MacMillan Publishing Company.

Young, T., & McClean, S. (2008). A critical look at Lean Thinking in Healthcare. *Quality and Safety in Health Care, 17*, 382–386.

CHAPTER 4

Delivering Agile and Person-centred Care

Abstract This chapter first briefly reviews agility from the perspective of its manufacturing origins. The review is extended to an agile supply chain perspective which highlights the need for flexibility and responsiveness. Here we recognise that the research on agile healthcare is limited; therefore we draw on two approaches that are promoting a flexible approach to healthcare. First, we examine the popularity of person-centred care (PCC) and the ability to put patients at the centre of their care. Second, we link this discussion around flexibility in the delivery of healthcare to the co-production agenda, which relates to value-based improvement. We analyse the application of agility within the context of other sectors.

Keywords Lean · Agile · Healthcare · Supply chain · Co-production · Person-centred

Introduction

This chapter first reviews agility as an approach to managing uncertainty within manufacturing supply chains. Flexibility and quick response are key characteristics of an agile supply chain. Here we also examine the popularity of person-centred care (PCC) and the call for flexibility in the delivery of some healthcare services. The rhetoric surrounding PCC is reviewed and how this approach is being operationalised within healthcare. This discussion is linked with the co-production of healthcare which relates to value-based improvement. The learning from other sectors is analysed and considered within the context of healthcare systems. Here we distinguish between lean and agile but we do not revisit the academic debate of lean OR agile.

AGILITY—A MANUFACTURING PERSPECTIVE

Agility was first introduced in response to the levels of uncertainty and change that organisations were facing (Ismail and Sharifi 2006). The term "agile manufacturing" was coined by a group of 150 US industrialists in 1990 who were seeking to develop a new paradigm for manufacturing and formed the Agile Manufacturing Enterprise Forum affiliated to the Iacocca Institute at Lehigh University (Sanchez and Nagi 2001). Some believe there are similarities between lean manufacturing and "agile manufacturing" but there are several differences. Sanchez and Nagi (2001) note these as being:

- Lean manufacturing exists in a competitive environment with limited resources. It provides a toolbox of operational techniques in which to improve the use of these resources and overall performance.
- Agile manufacturing provides an overall strategy for an unpredictable environment of complexity and continual change. Agile focuses on the responding to the individual needs of the customer.

Like lean, several definitions of agility exist (e.g. Christopher 2000; Aitken et al. 2002) but the ability to adapt to change in the environment, whether it originates from customers, competitors or stakeholders, is a key component of all definitions. Agility can be defined as "a business wide capability that embraces organisational structures, information systems, logistics processes and, in particular, mind-sets. A key characteristic of an agile organisation is flexibility" (Christopher 2000, p. 37). Sarkis (2001) states that a defining feature of agility is the ability to compete in a state of dynamic and continuous change. Hence, flexibility is a key characteristic of an agile organisation (Towill and Christopher 2002). Interestingly, agility did not receive attention for some time after the introduction of lean (Naylor et al. 1999). This may be due to the popularity of management books such as the *Machine that Changed the World* and *Lean Thinking*, whereas much of the writing on agile manufacturing appeared in academic journals which were perhaps less accessible to managers.

The origins of agile can be traced back to Flexible Manufacturing Systems (FMSs), which were initially aligned to the introduction of automation, designed to enable rapid changeovers to support greater responsiveness to changes in product mix or volume. Later this was extended to the wider business context (Nagel and Dove 1991) when agility was perceived as a mechanism to improve delivery of products. The core characteristics of agile manufacturing are shown in Table 4.1 along with an adaptation for healthcare services.

Table 4.1 Characteristics of agile manufacturing and agile healthcare

Activity	Agile manufacturing characteristics	Activity	Agile healthcare characteristics
Marketing	Customer enriching, individualised combination of products and services	Commissioning	Co-produced Patient/person-centredness
Production	Ability to produce goods & services to customer orders in variable lot sizes	Delivery of care	Ability to deliver care to patient demand and expectation
Design	Holistic methodology integrating suppliers, business processes, customers and products use and disposal	Service design	Holistic methodology integrating healthcare providers, business processes, commissioners & patients
Organisation	Ability to synthesise new productive capabilities from expertise of people and physical facilities regardless of their internal or external location	Organisation	Ability to synthesise new productive capabilities from expertise of people and physical facilities regardless of their internal or external location
Management	Emphasis of leadership, support, motivation and trust	Management	Emphasis of leadership (clinical and management), support, motivation and trust
People	Knowledgeable, skilled and innovative employees	People	Specialised, skilled, knowledgeable, and innovative employees

Source: Adapted from Goldman et al. (1995) and Towill and Christopher (2002).

Agility from a Supply Chain Perspective

The agile manufacturing system was first considered to be a business-wide concept. However, Christopher (2000) suggested in order to be "truly agile" then agility had to be at a supply chain level rather than with individual organisations. He referred to the "extended enterprise," which required the blurring or organisational boundaries, collaborative relationships built of trust and commitment, sharing of information and process integration. Christopher (2000) considered the supply chain, where a confederation of suppliers and customers are inked together as a network, as a key ingredient of agility.

Given our discussion in Chap. 3 we can also draw comparisons between the distinguishing attributes of lean and agile supply (see Fig. 4.1). This application is within a product-related supply chain environment but we believe it can be translated to have a meaningful contribution to the design of patient pathways. Here we propose some defining attributes for lean healthcare and agile healthcare supply (see Fig. 4.2). Later in the study we attempt to move this translation closer to the context of the two cases being addressed.

As noted above agility, as an approach to improving healthcare services, has received little attention from academics and practitioners alike. This next section aims to explain how agility links to existing concepts and approaches to quality improvement that are present in healthcare.

Person-Centred Care

To understand how improvement using agile principles can be linked with the growing movement of patient-centred care we must first try and outline what is meant by PCC. PCC has become a popular concept in healthcare and has exerted considerable influence on policy makers, practitioners and academics (McCormack 2004). Currently it is still ill-defined and terms such as "client", "patient", and "PCC" are used interchangeably. In 2000 Nay et al. predicted "client-centredness" would be the "watchword" for quality care in the twenty-first century. This insight was a result of the global trends associated with gerontic nursing and the new approaches to working with older people in various health and social care environments, including long-term care (Henderson and Vesperi 1995), rehabilitation (Nolan et al. 1997), learning disability (Williams and Grant 1998) and

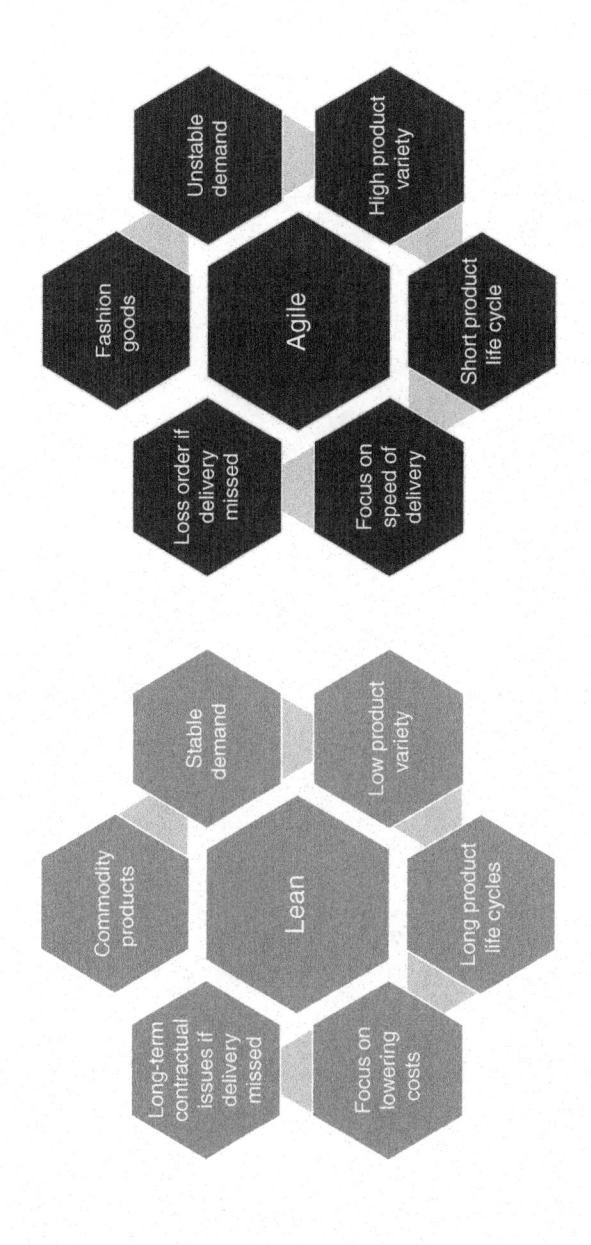

Fig. 4.1 Distinguishing attributes of lean and agile supply. (*Source:* Adapted from Mason-Jones and Towill (1997))

50　IMPROVING HEALTHCARE OPERATIONS

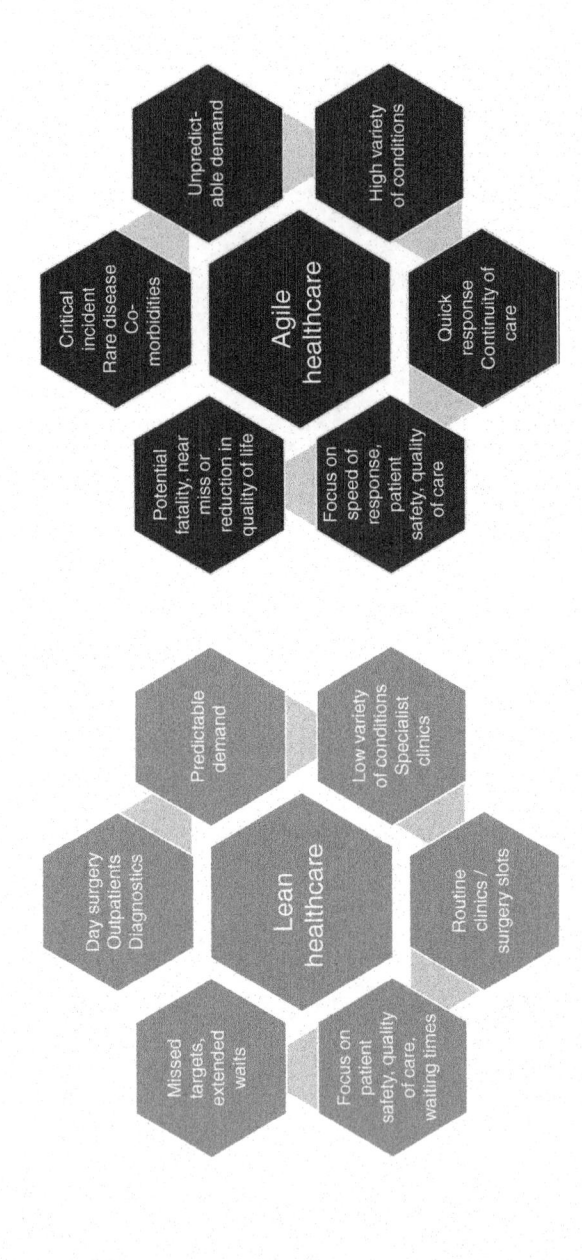

Fig. 4.2 Distinguishing attributes of lean healthcare and agile healthcare supply. (*Source:* Adapted from Mason-Jones and Towill (1997))

dementia care (Kitwood 1997). It was the latter area that provided a new sense of direction and purpose for practitioners.

The Health Foundation (2014) in the UK published a timeline for PCC, which attributes the term "patient-centred" to the works of an American psychologist, Carl Rogers. Other key contributions to PCC include in the late 1980s the establishment of the Foundation of Informed Decision Making in the US followed by the Chronic Care Model, which promoted the need for a proactive approach to healthcare, the basis of the Health Foundation's co-creation programme (Health Foundation 2014). To help bring some clarity to PCC several models have been developed which focus on person-centred nursing. For example, McCormack (2004) identifies four core components of person-centred nursing:

1. Relationships—the relationship between the nurse and patient is critical for successful outcomes.
2. Social world—the ability to adapt the context of care to create a caring environment that fits the needs of the person.
3. Place—the need to evaluate the environment and how this needs to be adapted to deliver person-centred care, not just the physical space and artefacts, but also softer elements such as systems of decision-making, staff relationships, organisational systems, power differentials and the potential of the organisation to tolerate innovate practices and risk taking.
4. Self-respect for values is integral to person-centred care. "Values" in this context refer to personal principles. Different to "value", in relation to improvement which is often described as a measurable outcome of some activity.

Understanding value is integral to PCC but pressures of everyday nursing may not allow this approach to prevail—hence, some doubt if PCC can be achieved and question whether it's simply an evangelical notion (Packer 2000). The general principles of co-producing value-based healthcare are integral to what is trying to be achieved by PCC.

Co-designing and Co-producing Health

Similar to PCC, the co-production agenda is gathering momentum within the healthcare arena. Unlike PCC, this does not seem to be a nurse-led phenomenon and is being embraced by all healthcare professionals. Critics might say, traditionally, healthcare services have always recognised the need for some kind of partnership with patients. It is the attention this has been given more recently in policy and organisational documentation that has promoted this as something central to improving healthcare. For example, in the US the Center for Medicare Services identifies patient and family engagement as a pillar in its efforts to improve healthcare (McCannon and Berwick 2011). Similarly, in social care participatory delivery of services is actively sought by policy makers (Cayton 2004; Needham and Carr 2009). Co-production is seen as a model of service delivery which should result in a positive impact on service users (patients) and on wider social systems (Realpe and Wallace 2010).

Some scholars propose that there is a continuum of perspectives on co-production which includes user involvement being "added into" the operational process of service delivery, as well as higher levels of co-production where the consumption and production of the service are taking place at the same point (Osborne et al. 2015). There is still confusion over the similarities and differences between co-production and co-design and how the latter impacts on this continuum.

If we consider co-production within the context of improvement, understanding value from the perspective of the user/consumer should be central to any (re)design activity and very often the starting point. Co-production is described as the concept which has profound implications for improving healthcare quality, safety and value (Batalden et al. 2015, p. 1). Drawing on multiple disciplines Batalden et al. (2015) helpfully discuss the theoretical underpinnings of co-production and how these have expanded our understanding of the notion. They argue that the domain of public services administration and management is particularly helpful and relevant.

Improvement Cycles

In healthcare we have seen an upward trend in the use of improvement models and cycles. Langley et al.'s (2009) model of improvement (see Fig. 4.3) has featured as a popular framework for improving healthcare processes and systems. The PDSA cycle is central to this model. As noted earlier this has also gained traction but not without some fidelity issues in relation to its use (see Reed and Card 2016) particularly around the planning element of the cycle. Here we introduce the concept of an agile methodology which originates from the world of IT and software development (Poppendieck and Poppendieck 2003). We believe there is

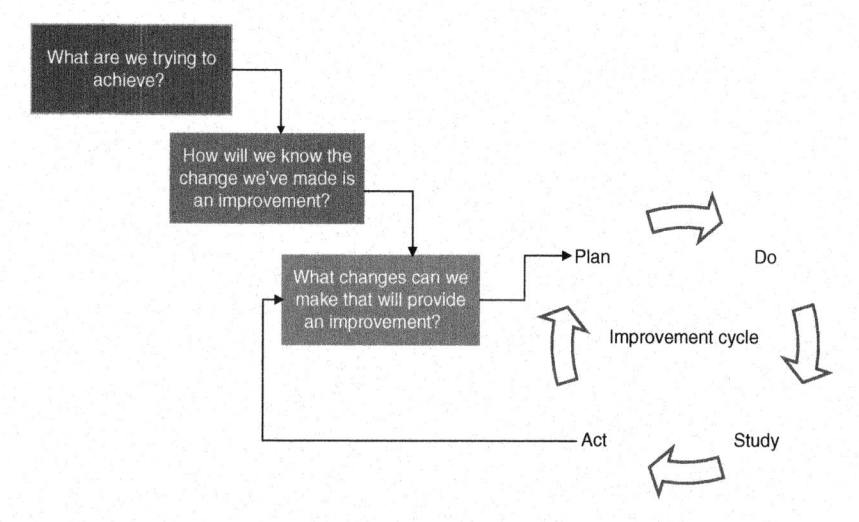

```
┌─────────────────┐
│ What are we trying to │
│     achieve?    │
└────────┬────────┘
         │
         ▼
    ┌─────────────────┐
    │ How will we know the │
    │ change we've made is │
    │  an improvement?│
    └────────┬────────┘
             │
             ▼
        ┌─────────────────┐
        │ What changes can we │
        │ make that will provide │
        │  an improvement?│
        └─────────────────┘
```

Fig. 4.3 Model for improvement. (*Source*: Adapted from Langley et al. (2009))

an opportunity in which to strengthen existing efforts in the use of improvement models and cycles. The agile methodology provides a structured approach with clear design features that would enable healthcare practitioners to ensure test cycles are completed in a timely manner with appropriate resources. The flexibility associated with the agile methodology could assist with unpacking the complexities of operationalising and managing healthcare improvement, particularly when improvement programmes span various healthcare providers and services.

In Table 4.2 we propose how the PDSA cycle and the agile methodology could be combined and employed within an improvement intervention or programme. The sprints and scrums used in the agile methodology provide the pace and reinforce the feedback loops so often missing in the execution of the PDSA cycle. As noted by Reed and Card (2016) the cyclical nature of the PDSA is often lost, and teams find it difficult to enact one cycle before resources start to drift elsewhere or are pulled to other priorities.

Conclusions

This chapter has reviewed agile from two perspectives. First, the traditional manufacturing view of a system being flexible in its response to market conditions and customer requirements. Much of this discussion was

Table 4.2 Combining the PDSA cycle and agile methodology

PDSA	Agile methodology
Plan	Form motivated self-organising team
	Define the problem (from customer's perspective) and appropriate measures for improvement
	Engage stakeholders and explain agile methodology
	Establish mechanisms for sprints and scrums
	Develop evidence to support proposed improvement intervention
Do	Test intervention
	Maintain face-to-face conversations with team and key stakeholders
	Establish regular sprint and scrum meetings to maintain and sustain the pace of improvement
	Focus attention on technical and operational excellence (do not let focus drift)
	Collect data and report measures frequently based on new practices/ intervention
	Create and reflect on feedback loops
Study	Review progress against measures and desired outcomes
	Reflect on and adapt intervention if needed
	Create positive response to any changes required
	Ensure feedback loops are appropriate in time and detail
Act	Use sprint and scrums to drive forward next cycle of change or adaptation of the intervention
	Review measures to ensure they will capture the change appropriately
	Continue with daily cooperation with the team and regular collaboration with key stakeholders

Source: Compiled by the author

related to product-related examples. We expand this to consider agility within the confines of a supply chain, which is more appropriate to the design of patient pathways.

In addition, we have reviewed two concepts, PCC and co-production that have recently been popularised in healthcare. Both concepts are concerned with putting patients at the centre of healthcare services and being flexible in how care is delivered. Although these are reviewed here in conjunction with agility, lean also promotes customer value being the driver for change and improvement. It was the flexibility angle of PCC and co-production that prompted the positioning of the discussion here.

Lean principles have underpinned many of the NHS improvement programmes (e.g. Productive Ward, Transforming Care). We propose that agility might offer an alternative or complementary approach to improvement and architecture of healthcare systems. Terminology needs to be translated and principles adapted to fit the healthcare environment.

We have also considered agile in relation to the project planning methodology, which originates from software development, in the context of improvement. It is evident there are parallels between this methodology and the well-known PDSA cycle and model of improvement used in healthcare. Hence, we propose these two approaches could be combined in order to provide a more robust approach in which to undertake improvement.

REFERENCES

Aitken, J., Christopher, M., & Towill, D. (2002). Understanding, implementing and exploiting agility and leanness. *International Journal of Logistics Research and Applications*, 5(1), 59–74.

Batalden, M., Batalden, P., Margolis, P., Seid, M., Armstrong, G., Opipari-Arrigan, L., & Hartung, H. (2015). Coproduction of healthcare service. *BMJ Quality & Safety*. Published online First: 16th September 2015.

Cayton, H. (2004). Patient-engagement and patient decision-making in England. Paper presented at the Improving Quality of Health Care in the United States and the United Kingdom: Strategies for Change and Action.

Christopher, M. (2000). The Agile supply chain. *Industrial Marketing Management*, 29(29), 37–44.

Goldman, S., Nagel, R., & Preiss, K. (1995). *Agile competitors and virtual organizations*. New York: van Nostrand Reinhold.

Henderson, J. A., & Vesperi, M. D. (1995). *The culture of long term care: Nursing home ethnography*. New York: Bergin and Garvey.

Ismail, H., & Sharifi, H. (2006). A balanced approach to building agile supply chains. *International Journal of Physical Distribution & Logistics Management*, 36(6), 431–444.

Kitwood, T. (1997). On being a person. In T. Kitwood (Ed.), *Dementia reconsidered: The person comes first* (pp. 7–19). Milton Keynes: Open University Press.

Langley, G. L., Nolan, K. M., Nolan, T. W., Norman, C. L., & Provost, L. P. (2009). *The improvement guide: A practical approach to enhancing organizational performance* (2nd Edition). San Francisco: Jossey Bass.

Mason-Jones, R., & Towill, D. R. (1997). Information enrichment: Designing the supply chain for competitive advantage. *Supply Chain Management*, 2(4), 137–148.

McCannon, J., & Berwick, D. (2011). A new frontier in patient safety. *Journal of the American Medical Association*, 305, 2221–2222.

McCormack, B. (2004). Person-centredness in gerontological nursing: An overview of the literature. *International Journal of Older People Nursing*, 13(3a), 31–38.

Nagel, R., & Dove, R. (1991). *21st century manufacturing enterprise strategy: An industry-led view*. Darby: Diane Publishing.

Nay, R., Rowell, G., & Hock, S. (2000). *Nursing care of older people: developments and innovations internationally*. Geneva: International Council of Nurses.

Naylor, J. B., Naim, M., & Berry, D. (1999). Leagility: Integrating the lean and agile manufacturing paradigms in the total supply chain. *International Journal of Production Economics*, 62(1/2), 107–108.

Needham, C., & Carr, S. (2009). *SCIE research briefing 31: Co-production: An emerging evidence base for adult social care transformation*. London: Social Care Institute for Excellence. Available from http://www.scie.org.uk/publications/briefings/briefing31/ [Accessed June 20, 2016]

Nolan, M. R., Booth, A., & Nolan, J. (1997). *New directions in rehabilitation: Exploring the nursing contribution*. London: Research Reports Series No. 6. English National Board for Nursing, Midwifery and Health Visiting.

Osborne, S., Radnor, Z., Vidal, I., & Kinder, T. (2015). The SERVICE framework: A public service-dominant approach to sustainable public services. *British Journal of Management*, 26(3), 424–438.

Packer, T. (2000). Does person-centred care exist? *Journal of Dementia Care*, 8, 19–21.

Poppendieck, M., & Poppendieck, T. (2003). *Lean software development: An agile toolkit*. New Jersey: Addison-Wesley Professional. ISBN:978-0-321-15078-3.

Realpe, A., & Wallace, L. (2010). *What is co-production?* London: The Health Foundation.

Reed, J., & Card, A. (2016). The problem with Plan-Do-Study-Act Cycles. *BMJ Quality and Safety*, 25(3), 147–152.

Sanchez, L. M., & Nagi, R. (2001). A review of agile manufacturing systems. *International Journal of Production Research*, 39(16), 3561–3600.

Sarkis, J. (2001). Benchmarking for agility. *Benchmarking: An International Journal*, 8(2), 88–107.

The Health Foundation. (2014). Person-centred care timeline, Health Foundation. Available at http://personcentredcare.health.org.uk/resources/person-centred-care-timeline [Accessed February 7, 2016]

Towill, D. R., & Christopher, M. (2002). The supply chain strategy conundrum: To be lean or agile? *International Journal of Logistics Research and Applications*, 3(3), 299–309.

Williams, B., & Grant, G. (1998). Defining "people-centredness": Making the implicit explicit. *Health and Social Care in the Community*, 6, 84–94.

CHAPTER 5

Leanness Plus Agility = Leagility

Abstract This chapter examines the literature on leagility, which is largely premised on manufacturing examples. Here we consider how to bring together lean and agile, two improvement paradigms, to provide an approach that is useful for the (re)design of patient pathways. The chapter explores how decoupling points (DPs) have been used within supply chain design and we propose how these concept can be used in healthcare. We provide a review of the limited literature on leagility in healthcare and propose a conceptual framework where lean, agile and leagile may be used to help deliver seamless healthcare services and improve the design of patient care pathways.

Keywords Leagility · Lean · Agile · Healthcare · Supply chain · Decoupling

Introduction

This chapter examines the literature on leagility, which is largely premised on manufacturing examples. It also illustrates how few studies have considered leagility within the context of healthcare and more specifically the design of care pathways. A conceptual framework is provided that will be empirically tested through the use of case research presented in Chaps. 7 and 8.

As highlighted in Chaps. 3 and 4, there is little consensus on defining lean and agile. We have considered these approaches individually in relation to their roles in manufacturing systems and supply chains. There are some scholars (e.g. ReVelle 2004) who believe there is a need for organisations to implement lean before progressing to agile; in other words lean is a prerequisite to agile. Other scholars (e.g. Naylor et al. 1999; Christopher 2000) advocate a hybrid approach which we explore further in this chapter.

Leanness and Agility—Leagility

Chapters 3 and 4 have introduced two improvement and supply chain paradigms—lean and agility. Here we are building on these discussions to consider how we might bring these together to provide an approach that is useful for the (re)design of patient pathways.

To remind ourselves of the distinction between these two concepts we simply draw on *Webster's Dictionary* definitions where "lean" is described as "containing little fat" and "agile" is defined as "nimble" (Towill and Christopher 2002, p. 302). After considerable academic debate Naylor et al. (1999) recognised that lean and agile are not contrasting ideas but in fact made a case for both approaches. They termed this combined or hybrid approach as leagility. The choice of whether to have a lean, agile or leagile supply chain will depend on market conditions and customer expectations (see Fig. 5.1). Factors such as the levels of product variation and availability will have an impact on the design of the supply chain.

Christopher (2000, p. 40) recognised there are occasions where a "pure" agile or "pure" lean strategy might be the most appropriate for an organisation and their supply chains, but he also proposed there could be occasions where a hybrid (leagility) approach may be needed which combines the two strategies. Christopher (ibid) advocates the need for leagility when a mixed portfolio of products and markets exists, which is not so much about a supply chain being lean OR agile but the need to be lean part of the time and agile for the remainder. As we note above such decisions need to consider the market conditions in relation to the predictability of demand, levels of variety and volumes. Previous studies have identified a list of distinguishing attributes of lean, agile and leagility supply chains (see Naylor et al. 1999; Mason-Jones et al. 2000; Olhager 2003; Bruce et al. 2004).

The overall aim of leagility is to leverage synergies in both leanness and agility through their decoupling via strategic use of stock in the

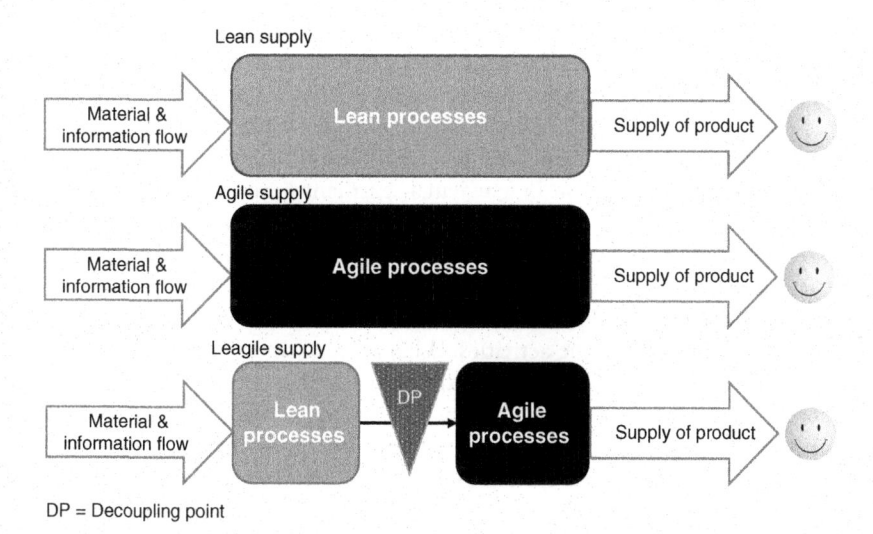

Fig. 5.1 Lean, agile or leagile? Matching your supply chain to the marketplace. (*Source*: Adapted from Towill et al., 2000)

product delivery process (Naim and Gosling 2011). Two identifiers of lean are a source to lower costs and the ability to do more with less or the same which increases rates of efficiency, whereas agile is seen as a source of differentiation and being able to respond rapidly to changes in demand, hence increasing effectiveness (Naylor et al. 1999; Christopher 2000).

Leagile Supply Chains

Much of the discussion around combining lean and agile has been at a supply chain level and given the focus of the study is pathway design this seems an appropriate perspective to take. Christopher (2000) helpfully makes the distinction of where in the supply chain design lean and agile are likely to be most appropriate. He argues a lean approach is most suited to the upstream activities which are based on forecasts and an agile approach downstream where activities are based on known demand and are visible (Christopher 2000). Christopher (ibid) cites Zara, the Spanish fashion clothing company, as employing a hybrid strategy. He describes the company as having developed one of the most effective quick-response systems in the garment industry. The company's strategy involves the high volume, cost-efficient activities (such as dying, cutting, labelling and packaging) being managed in-house, and all other manufacturing activities (such as the labour-intensive finishing stages) being outsourced to a network of small subcontractors who specialise in different areas of the manufacturing process or in particular garments. Some materials and fabrics are also held in "greige" (un-dyed and unprinted) to enable the company to respond quickly should the demand for a particular garment be higher than expected.

Following lean principles enables a system to reduce variation, standardise and remove non-value activities. Where this becomes more difficult to achieve then a more adaptive and flexible approach is needed. As discussed here both approaches can be combined in one system as long as it is clear where the movement (also known as the decoupling) from one approach to the other occurs. As we noted earlier some scholars believe lean is a prerequisite to agile.

Naim and Gosling (2011) usefully review the literature on lean, agile and leagility. Some examples of the application of leagility include. Krishnamurthy and Yauch (2007), who from a corporate perspective, demonstrate the decoupling point (DP) is not limited to physical flow of products, but decoupling can be used between functions, in this case between the sales and services Group, which is agile and market focused, and the production units, which are lean and production focused. Another example by Wikner and Rudberg (2005) conceptualises agility in an engineering environment and distinguishes between engineer-to-order and engineer-to-stock. This latter example, along with others (e.g. Naim and Barlow 2003), conceptualises how decoupling and leagility may be applied outside a manufacturing environment. Interestingly, the discussion of lean and agile is rarely present within healthcare (Aronsson et al. 2011), but Naim and Gosling (2011) propose healthcare as one of the areas for further study.

Decoupling Points

In the section above we have introduced the notion of decoupling. In manufacturing when shifting from lean to agile or vice versa there is what is known as a DP. There is an extant literature base on this subject. For the purpose of this study it is useful here to illustrate the various DPs that might be applied within a manufacturing environment (see Fig. 5.2).

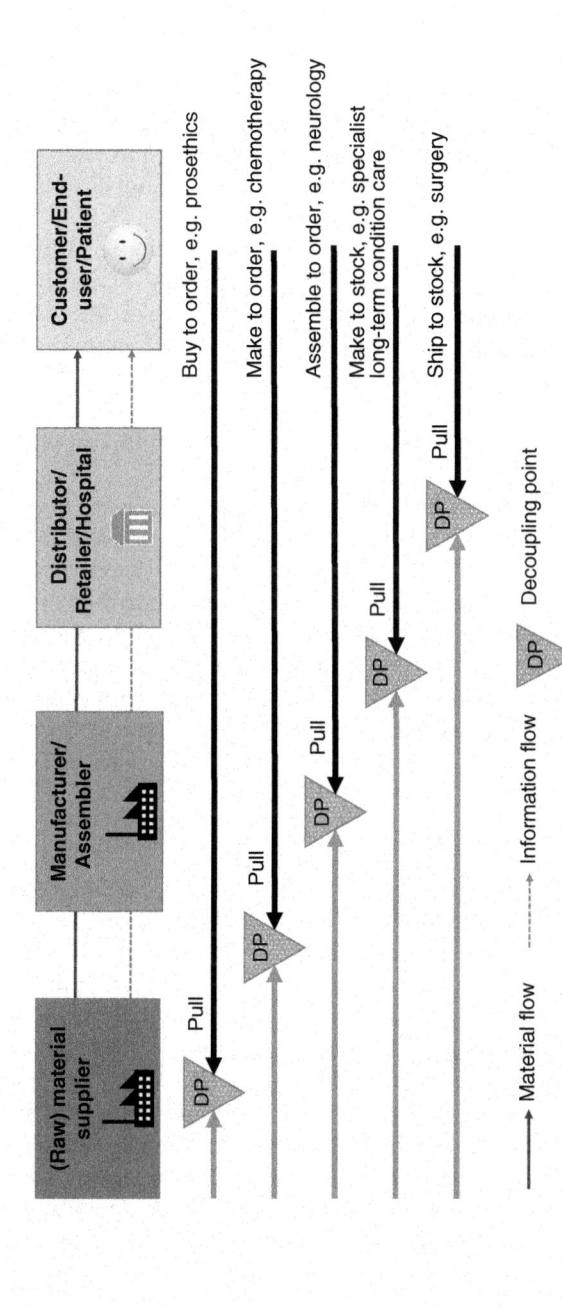

Fig. 5.2 Supply chain strategies and positioning of decoupling points. (*Source*: Adapted from Naylor et al. (1999))

Within a supply chain the DP can be represented as a material DP (MDP) or an information DP (IDP) where the customer order meets an internally forecast-driven plan (Banomyong et al. 2008; Towill and Christopher 2002). Research has investigated the strategic benefits and the identification of both DPs to support the application of lean and agile in various business contexts ranging from food production to global supply chains (Banerjee et al. 2012; Akkerman et al. 2010).

Christopher (2000) makes the distinction between the MDP and the IDP. The MDP relates to the strategic positioning of inventory in a generic form (e.g. un-dyed material as noted in the Zara example). Ideally this point should be located as close to the customer/end consumer (or downstream) as possible. The postponement of this decision can significantly improve the level of responsiveness to the customer. In contrast the IDP should be located as far upstream in the supply chain as possible to provide details of "real" customer demand.

We examine five different product-based supply chains to demonstrate the various points at which a DP might be placed (Naylor et al. 1999). We attempt to translate these five strategies to a health service environment by providing healthcare examples that have similar attributes to those described for each of the five strategies (see Table 5.1). We recognise that the terminology used here, such as "stock", may not be applicable to all of the healthcare examples. We have not made the distinction between MDPs and IDPs or considered what these mean to patient flows. In this study we intend to investigate further the use of DPs in pathway design.

Front-Office and Back-Office Activities

Another way of defining decoupling in service operations takes into consideration front-office and back-office differentiation. For example, decoupling can be defined as "breaking a process into its component back- and front-office activities, segregating those activities into distinct back- and front-office jobs, and, usually, geographically separating the back and front offices" (Metters and Vargas 2000, p. 664). Front-office activities are those that are customer facing and the back-office processes are removed from customer view and can be designed for efficiency through the use of lean thinking. One way to improve efficiency is to identify and shift additional activities to the back office (Chase and Tansik 1983). In terms of healthcare a front-office activity would be some interaction with a patient or relative (e.g. patient arrival at an

Table 5.1 Supply chain strategies and healthcare examples

Supply chain strategy	Healthcare examples
1. *Buy-to-order* is appropriate if all products are unique and the consumer is prepared to accept long lead times and the demand for products is highly variable. Holding stock would run the risk of becoming obsolete.	Prosthetics are all bought to order as each one is unique to the patient.
2. *Make-to-order* is able to change to different products as long as they are made from the same raw materials. It will also cope with varied locations, volumes and product mixes. The consumer is likely to have to accept a considerable wait to get the product they want. There will be a high level of customisation.	Chemotherapy treatment is based on the same drugs but the combination of drugs and dosage will vary depending on the patient's condition and treatment regime.
3. *Assemble-to-order* supply chain structure is where customisation is postponed until as late as possible. The supply chain can respond to a varied product mix from within a range of products, whether customised or not. The lead time will be reduced considerably.	This relates to person-centred care where standard interventions are offered to the patient as and when needed within their trajectory of care. The care of neurological conditions is likely to fit into this category.
4. The *make-to-stock* strategy means that the supply chain can cope with demands in varied locations but requires a steady demand of a standard product.	The role of specialist nurses could fit in the category. Especially if working in various locations, for example, community, GP practices, hospital clinics, etc. They deliver a specialised service to a specific group of patients, for example, long-term conditions such as diabetes, cardiac and respiratory.
5. The *ship-to-stock* strategy provides a standard product in fixed locations. This strategy relies on being able to forecast demand accurately. It is critical to hold the correct level of stock to minimise the risk of stock-outs and overstocks.	This strategy seems to fit a surgical environment. Minor operations and day-case surgery are standard procedures located in theatres or clinic rooms. The availability of equipment, expertise and materials is important along with the scheduling of the theatre/clinic time and preparation of the patient.

Source: Compiled by the author

outpatient reception or clinic) and a back-office activity would be void of this interaction (e.g. testing of blood samples).

Leagility in Healthcare

As noted previously, the discussion of leagility is rarely present within healthcare particularly in relation to patient flows (Aronsson et al. 2011; Olsson and Aronsson 2015). Aronsson et al. (2011) suggest that leagile when related to patients is not practical as decoupling strategies using concepts such as postponement cannot exist due to the patient being involved in the entire process. In terms of services, however, queues and waiting lists are often utilised to decouple stages and manage capacity constraints (Rahimnia and Moghadasian 2010) leading to "inventories of patients". Within healthcare this is exemplified by accident and emergency (A&E) services delivering patients to surgical teams. Information flows also have their challenges between stages of the healthcare supply chain and are often vulnerable to issues leading to quality and service problems (Manser and Foster 2011). The movement of patients and information between autonomous stages of the healthcare supply chain is of critical importance to health and well-being (Meijboom et al. 2011; Manser and Foster 2011).

One of the few studies to focus on patient flow rather than material flows, Olsson and Aronsson (2015) identified lean, agile and leagile actions were taken by a Swedish University hospital to manage their variable acute patient flows. These actions were taken at both hospital and departmental levels. The lean categories identified by the authors included managing external variation, reduced need for a resource and standardised patient flow. The agile categories included extending the use of a resource, altering the amount of a resource ahead of demand, and altering the amount of a resource as a response to demand. The authors suggest hospitals should not solely focus on implementing lean, but to extend their improvement efforts to include agile, and by cleverly combining these two approaches then leagile responses can be formed. This study has shown that lean, agile and leagility can make a contribution to improving the delivery of healthcare. We extend this research by moving beyond the boundary of one organisation (hospital) to focus on two pathways that include primary (community) and secondary (hospital) care.

We build upon Parnaby and Towill's (2008) seamless healthcare system by proposing a conceptual model (see Fig. 5.3) which depicts how lean

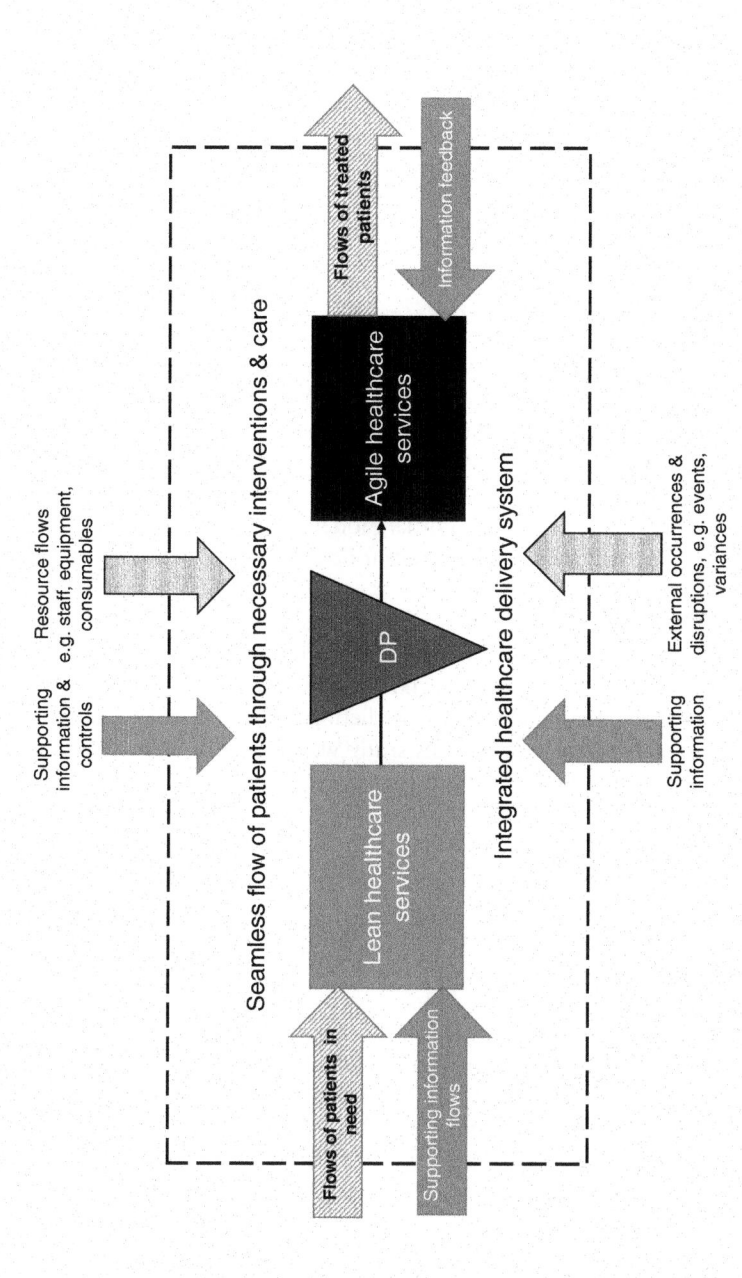

Fig. 5.3 Conceptual model: Leagility in the design and integration of healthcare systems. (*Source*: Adapted from Parnaby and Towill (2008))

and agile may both be employed. We have located lean upstream, similar to the positioning used in manufacturing, where forward planning helps to manage this part of the pathway or healthcare system. Agility is then located downstream to respond to the needs of the patient. It is possible that more than one DP could exist within a pathway which spans primary and secondary healthcare. In Chaps. 7 and 8, using empirical data, we will test this conceptual thinking and discuss the results in Chap. 9.

Conclusions

In this chapter we have briefly reviewed the concept of leagilty and considered its application within a manufacturing and a healthcare environment. We recognise the terminology employed within the area of supply chains, DPs and leagility, may need some translation before any meaningful comparisons or application can be made to patient pathway design. We have developed a conceptual model to extend the DP thinking to healthcare and provide some guidance for our empirical work which will be presented in Chaps. 7 and 8.

Lean, agile and leagility provide alternatives in which to view supply chain architecture and quality improvement. Identifying where decoupling points are best placed may be more challenging in healthcare given the difficulties often associated with predicting patient demand and personalising (customising) care. In this study we intend to explore what is transferrable to the design of patient pathways.

References

Akkerman, R., Van Der Meer, D., & Van Donk, P. D. (2010). Make to stock and mix to order: Choosing intermediate products in the food processing industry. *International Journal of Production Research, 48*(12), 3475–3492.

Aronsson, H., Abrahamsson, M., & Spens, K. (2011). Developing lean and agile health care supply chains. *Supply Chain Management, 16*(3), 176–183.

Banerjee, A., Sarkar, B., & Mukhopadhyay, S. (2012). Multiple decoupling point paradigms in a global supply chain syndrome: A relational analysis. *International Journal of Production Research, 50*(11), 3051–3065.

Banomyong, R., Veerkachen, V., & Supatn, N. (2008). Implementing leagility in reverse logistics channels. *International Journal of Logistics Research and Applications, 11*(1), 31–47.

Bruce, M., Daly, L., & Towers, N. (2004). Lean or agile: A solution for supply chain management in the textiles and clothing industry?. *International Journal of Operations & Production Management, 24*(2), 151–170.

Chase, R., & Tansik, D. (1983). The customer contact model for organisation design. *Management Science, 29*(9), 1037–1050.

Christopher, M. (2000). The Agile supply chain: Competing in volatile markets. *Industrial Marketing Management, 29*(1), 37–44.

Krishnamurthy, R., & Yauch, C. (2007). Leagile manufacturing: A proposed corporate infrastructure. *International Journal of Operations & Production Management, 27*(6), 588–604.

Manser, T., & Foster, S. (2011). Effective handover communication: An overview of research and improvement efforts. *Best Practice & Research Clinical Anaesthesiology, 25*(2), 181–191.

Mason-Jones, R., Naylor, B., & Towill, D.R. (2000). Lean, agile or leagile? Matching your supply chain to the marketplace. *International Journlal of Production Research, 38*(17), 4061–4070.

Meijboom, B., Schmidt-Bakx, S., & Westert, G. (2011). Supply chain management practices for improving patient-orientated care. *Supply Chain Management: An International Journal, 16*(3), 166–175.

Metters, R., & Vargas, V. (2000). A typology of decoupling strategies in mixed services. *Journal of Operations Management, 18*(6), 663–682.

Naim, M., & Barlow, J. (2003). An innovative supply chain strategy for customized housing. *Construction Management and Economics, 21*, 593–602.

Naim, M., & Gosling, J. (2011). On leanness, agility and leagile supply chains. *International Journal of Production Economics, 131*, 342–354.

Naylor, J. B., Naim, M., & Berry, D. (1999). Leagility: Integrating the lean and agile manufacturing paradigms in the total supply chain. *International Journal of Production Economics, 62*(1/2), 107–108.

Olhager, J. (2003). Strategic positioning of the order pentration point. *International Journal of Production Economics, 85*(3), 319–329.

Olsson, O., & Aronsson, H. (2015). Managing a variable acute patient flow – categorising the strategies. *Supply Chain Management: An international Journal, 20*(2), 113–127.

Parnaby, J., & Towill, D. R. (2008). Seamless healthcare delivery systems. *International Journal of Health Care Quality Assurance, 21*(3), 249–273.

Rahimnia, F., & Moghadasian, M. (2010). Supply chain leagility in professional services: How to apply decoupling point concept in healthcare delivery system. *Supply Chain Management: An International Journal, 15*(1), 80–91.

ReVelle, J. (2004). *Quality essentials: A reference guide from A to Z*. Milwaukee: ASQ Quality Press.

Towill, D. R., Childerhouse, P., & Disney, S. M. (2000). Speeding up the progress curve towards effective supply chain management. *International Journal of Supply Chain Management, 5*(43), 122–130.

Towill, D. R., & Christopher, M. (2002). The supply chain strategy conundrum: To be lean or agile?. *International Journal of Logistics Research and Applications, 3*(3), 299–309.

Wikner, J., & Rudberg, M. (2005). Integrating production and engineering perspectives on the customer order decoupling point. *International Journal of Operations & Production Management, 25*(7), 623–641.

CHAPTER 6

Methodology

Abstract This chapter details the methodological approach for the study. This qualitative research includes two cases which span multiple healthcare services and organisations. Through the use of experience-based interviews with patients, relatives and staff, focus groups, non-participant observations and validation workshops we examine the design and delivery of patient pathways. We focus on two long-term chronic conditions—chronic obstructive pulmonary disease (COPD) and Huntington's disease (HD). Ethical considerations are discussed along with limitations of the research. Details of the thematic analysis undertaken for the study are presented and an example of the coding framework is included.

Keywords: Qualitative case study · Pathway · Healthcare · Focus groups · Thematic analysis

Introduction

This chapter details the methodological approach for the study. This qualitative research includes two cases which span multiple services and organisations. The case selection details are given along with the data collection methods. Ethical considerations are presented along with limitations of the research.

© The Author(s) 2017
S.J. Williams, *Improving Healthcare Operations*,
DOI 10.1007/978-3-319-46913-3_6

Preparation and Understanding the Research Environment

Initially it was intended that this research should focus on the design of integrated care pathways (ICP) as described by de Bleser et al. (2006, p. 562): "a method for the patient care management of a well-defined group of patient during a well-defined period of time". Joosten et al. (2008) purport that ICPs are approaches that focus on quality improvement, especially for standardising and improving delivery processes. Similarly, Allen et al. (2009) report ICPs to be most effective when patient journeys are predictable. Hence, typically ICPs provide a documented trajectory or pathway for a specified condition.

When the search started for suitable pathways it soon became clear that ICPs are viewed by healthcare professionals and academics in very different ways. ICPs have been a useful approach to pathway design but operationalised in different ways with different outcomes. There was considerable interest in the study from potential sites but it was evident that the proposed ICPs were not always well defined or operationalised. In the end, two pathways were selected that could provide contrasting evidence: one being high volume, low variation, and the other, low volume and high variation.

Before conducting the research, a full NHS research ethics application was made. Approval was granted by the Research Ethics Committee. Approval was also sought from the Research and Development (R&D) Office of each organisation taking part in the study.

Study Design and Methods

This inductive and qualitative case research aims to provide a better understanding of the design of the patient pathway for two chronic conditions. Details are presented here of the pathways and participants, methods and analysis.

Selection of Care Pathways

Five healthcare organisations located in the UK agreed to participate in this case research. Two chronic disease pathways were selected for the study: chronic obstructive pulmonary disease (COPD) and Huntington's disease (HD). The selection of the two case pathways was intended to enable a comparison of the different needs of a common disease group to that of a rare disease group (Yin 2009). It was anticipated that the pathways would be different in the way they are designed and used and would provide a deeper insight into pathway design and the potential application of improvement approaches. These two conditions are clearly very different in terms of the number of people living with the disease (volume) and the complexity in relation to symptoms (variation); there is a real desire from staff and patients/relatives/carers to manage both conditions within the community and reduce avoidable admissions to hospital where possible. The requirements of the pathways are similar in that patients are looking for a joined-up approach to the provision of care across healthcare providers but clearly patient experiences will vary depending on the complexity of their condition. Given the above details of each of the two diseases, we propose to classify COPD in supply chain parlance as a "runner/repeater" activity and HD as a "stranger" condition. We will discuss these classifications in further detail during the analysis of the pathway data.

Chronic Obstructive Pulmonary Disease Pathway

For COPD it is estimated in the UK that there are more than 3 million people living with the condition, of which only about 900,000 have been diagnosed and an estimated 2 million people remain undiagnosed (Healthcare Commission 2006). Most patients are not diagnosed until they are in their fifties. COPD accounts for approximately 30,000 deaths per year.

The COPD pathway research will include primary and secondary care. The British Lung Foundation (BLF) developed an interactive pathway website which demonstrates the key components of care that COPD patients might require. The BLF state that they have designed the pathway by synthesising information, knowledge and best practice from across England. The pathway is intended to provide guidance to healthcare professionals and commissioners on how to provide the best care for people with COPD in their area. The BLF pathway is also for patients to check that they are getting the right care and to signpost them to wider care and support that is available. The pathway provides examples of best practice, links to BLF information and explains the National Institute of Health and Care Excellence (NICE) standards. The website also informs patients and carers about other types of care that are available which might help them to manage COPD more effectively.

Table 6.1 Inclusion and exclusion criteria for the selection of research participants

Inclusion criteria	Exclusion criteria
Male or female	Participants who are unable to consent for themselves
18 years of age or older	
Able to consent for themselves	
Caregiver or receiver (including relatives/carer) for the selected conditions	

Source: Author

Huntington's Disease Pathway

The second selected pathway is that for HD. It is estimated between 6,000 and 8,000 people within the UK have been diagnosed with HD (HD Association, 2012). This is a hereditary disorder of the central nervous system and usually develops in adulthood and can cause a wide range of symptoms.

The HD pathway will be profiled across organisational boundaries—for example, from a hospital-based disease clinic to a community-based complex care team specialising in HD. The HD Association has recently published the HD care pathway. This interactive pathway is posted on the HDA website with each category of the pathway providing additional information for patients and their families/carers. At a recent HDA Annual General Meeting and Family Conference family members and people with HD reported that having an understanding of the care pathway and knowing who to signpost it to would make dealing with the illness easier (Stanley 2014). The HD Association is now following up on this and other statements raised by the 240 conference attendees.

A summary of the inclusion and exclusion criteria for both cases is provided in Table 6.1.

Data Collection and Data Analysis

An information sheet for the study was given to all participants before observations or interviews were conducted. Consent was obtained from all participants involved in the study. Data were collected using the following methods.

Non-participant Observation

Pathway activities were observed at each study site. This involved observing consenting patients (and their companions) at routine clinics/outpatient appointments and during ward rounds. Anonymised field notes were recorded and subsequently the data were coded and analysed.

Semi-structured Interviews with Patients, Relatives/Carers and Staff Participants

Semi-structured experience-based interviews were conducted either at the patient's home or whilst at hospital and at the place of work for the healthcare professional.

- Patients and relatives/carers—20 patients and relatives (HD— 6 relatives and 2 patients and COPD—10 patients and 2 relatives) participated in the study.
- Healthcare professionals—interviews were conducted with 25 community and hospital healthcare professionals and managers which included the following:
  o COPD pathway—Specialist nurses, respiratory consultants and junior doctors, commissioners.
  o HD pathway— Psychologists, mental health nurses, occupational therapists, speech and language therapists and physiotherapists

The duration of the interviews ranged from 30 minutes to 90 minutes and focused on the experiences of those involved in delivering or receiving care. The interviews were audio-recorded and transcribed. The data were anonymised and analysed as detailed below.

A thematic analysis of the staff and patient data was conducted. In addition, mapping exercises of the selected pathways were completed and presented to patient groups for confirmation of accuracy.

Focus Groups

A focus group was held with COPD patients attending a pulmonary rehabilitation programme. All eighteen patients were invited to participate in the study; five agreed to take part in the focus group. The duration of the activity was 45 minutes. Similar to the semi-structured interviews, participants were asked to share their experiences of getting a daignosis through to managing their condition.

Validation of Results

The anonymised results of the study have been validated by presenting the findings at staff meetings and various patient and relative groups. Feedback received from these meetings has been used to finalise the results presented in the next two chapters.

Data Analysis

The unit of analysis is two existing patient pathways in a healthcare system, that is, a set of steps within and across organisations that deliver care for patients with either COPD or HD. A thematic analysis is used to analyse the field notes from the observations and the transcripts of the focus group and interviews (King 2004). This data triangulation (Patton 2002) provides a fuller and richer picture of the pathway design. The analysis also allows for the development of conceptual themes and clustering of these themes into broader groupings (Cassell and Symon 2004). Template analysis requires a list of codes or a "template" to be produced which represents themes identified in the textual data (King 1998). An initial template has been constructed which is based upon the research topic and the themes that emerged from reading the first few transcripts. The analysis is an iterative process and the themes are continually reviewed as the interviews continued. An extract of the thematic template which includes the sub-codes is shown in Table 6.2. Anonymous quotations are included in the reporting of the results.

Credibility and Rigour

Evaluating the quality of research is essential if findings are to be utilised in practice (Noble and Smith 2015). Qualitative research is often criticised for lack of scientific rigour (Rolfe 2006). There is much debate as to whether terms such as "validity", "reliability" and "generalisability" are appropriate to evaluate qualitative research. Lincoln and Guba (1985) offer alternative criteria for demonstrating rigour within qualitative research. Using these criteria, we demonstrate the strategies employed to demonstrate credibility of our research (see Table 6.3).

Table 6.2 Extract from the thematic framework

Themes	Codes	Sub-codes
Information flows	IT systems	Poor interface (staff participants commented, "systems don't talk to one another") Joined up (patients and relatives assumed all systems "spoke to one another")
	Professional to professional	Personal relationships (over a period of time staff participants build up personal knowledge of whom to contact) Incompatible systems (entry to patient records is made by profession) Broker—Specialist role (enables the flow of information)
	Professional to patient	Missing data/history (patients/relatives often provide missing data or information on medical history) Broker—Patient/relative (patient/relative often informs community healthcare professionals when admitted to hospital)

Table 6.3 Criteria and strategies employed to demonstrate credibility of research

Criteria to evaluate the credibility	Strategies employed
Truth value (validity)	The interviews were audio-recorded and transcribed verbatim. Able to regularly revisit these during the analysis process to ensure themes are true to the personal accounts given. Two patient groups and one group of healthcare professionals were invited to comment on the themes from the analysis. A reflective diary was kept by the lead author during the research which documented the research process and decisions made, for example, slight change of emphasis from definitions of pathways to how pathways are operationalised.
Consistency/neutrality (reliability)	The research process was documented from initial proposal and ethics approval through to data collection and analysis and reporting findings. Emerging themes continually reviewed.
Applicability (generalisability)	Context of the illustrative cases (e.g. pathway design of two conditions) provided in this chapter facilitates the conceptual model and the recommendations for further research for empirical testing in other conditions.

(Based on Lincoln and Guba 1985)

Conclusions

Initially, ICPs had been identified as the unit of analysis for this study. However, it soon became apparent that despite this being a popular approach to documenting pathway design, there was little consensus among healthcare professionals about definitions and implementation. Similarly, not all ICPs span community and primary care which was one of the areas this research intended to address. This narrow use of ICPs was a concern and hence the research was broadened to ensure patient pathways were observed from end to end—that is, from diagnosis to managing long-term care. As a result, the study became more explorative in nature and relied on experience-based interviews to map the pathways. We have discussed the methodological approach taken and the mixed methods used for this study. Details of the thematic analysis and coding framework are provided.

It was the intention to complete some quantitative analysis in relation to understanding the volume and variety of activity. Again some adjustments have been made to accommodate the lack of appropriate data. We revisit these methodological issues again in Chap. 10 where recommendations are made for future research which addresses these limitations.

The ability to negotiate the NHS ethics approval process is a real skill that takes time to develop, particularly if working from outside of medicine or healthcare sciences. Seeking expert assistance from a very early stage in the research process will help to position the research and negotiate the complexities of online systems, organisational research and development approval procedures and managing updates and amendments.

Often there is a need to be flexible in the way we conduct our research. This might be when and where interviews are conducted. The ability to reflect on the sensitivity of participants sharing their healthcare experiences must be at the forefront of the researcher's mind. It is important to have the appropriate debriefing and support mechanisms in place.

References

Allen, D., Gillen, E., & Rixson, L. (2009). Systematic review of the effectiveness of integrated care pathways: What works, for whom, in which circumstances? *International Journal of Evidence Based Healthcare, 7*, 61–74.

Cassell, C., & Symon, G. (Eds.). (2004). *Essential guide to qualitative methods in organisational research*. London: Sage Publications Ltd.

De Bleser, L., Depreitere, R., De Waele, K., Vanhaecht, K., Vlayen, J., & Sermeus, W. (2006). Defining pathways. *Journal of Nursing Management*, *14*(7), 553–563.

Healthcare Commission. (2006). *Clearing the air: A national study of chronic obstructive pulmonary disease*. London: Healthcare Commission.

Huntington's Disease Association. (2012). Available at http://hda.org.uk/hd [Accessed June 16, 2016].

Joosten, T., Bongers, I., & Meijboom, I. B. (2008). Care programmes and integrated care pathways. *International Journal of Health Care Quality Assurance*, *21*(5), 472–486.

King, N. (1998). Template analysis. In G. Symon & C. Cassell (Eds.), *Qualitative methods and analysis in organisational research*. London: Sage.

King, N. (2004). Using templates in the thematic analysis of text. In C. Cassell & G. Symon (Eds.), *Essential guide to qualitative methods in organisational research*. London: Sage.

Lincoln, Y. S., & Guba, E. G. (1985). *Naturalist enquiry*. Beverley Hills, CA: Sage Publications.

Noble, H., & Smith, J. (2015). Issues of validity and reliability of qualitative research. *Evidence Based Nursing*, *18*(2), 34–35.

Patton, M. (2002). *Qualitative education and research methods*. Thousand Oaks, CA: Sage Publication.

Rolfe, G. (2006). Validity, trustworthiness and rigour: Quality and the idea of qualitative research. *Journal of Advanced Nursing*, *53*, 304–310.

Stanley, C. (2014), Huntington's Disease Association.

Yin, R. (2009). *Case study research: Design and method* (4th edition). Thousand Oaks, CA: Sage Publications.

CHAPTER 7

Analysis of the COPD Pathway: Lean, Agile and Leagility

Abstract This chapter presents case research on the design of a long-term respiratory condition, chronic obstructive pulmonary disease (COPD), patient pathway. The case draws on the design of a service which spans three hospital sites and two commissioning groups in the UK. From conducting observations, focus groups, validation workshops and interviews with healthcare professionals, patients and relatives, the qualitative thematic analysis enables a detailed picture of existing services to be compiled. We provide illustrations of the current COPD pathway and sub-processes within the pathway, identifying patient, information, resource and emotional flows. We identify points in the pathway where lean, agile and leagility influence or may improve the design of the COPD patient pathway being studied.

Keywords Pathway · Patient · COPD · Flow · Lean · Agile

INTRODUCTION

This chapter presents the first of two case studies—this case focuses on the design of a long-term respiratory condition, chronic obstructive pulmonary disease (COPD) pathway, described by one of the staff participants as the "bread and butter of respiratory". The case draws on the design of a service which spans three hospital sites and two commissioning groups in the UK. From conducting non-participant observations, focus groups,

© The Author(s) 2017
S.J. Williams, *Improving Healthcare Operations*,
DOI 10.1007/978-3-319-46913-3_7

validation workshops and semi-structured interviews with healthcare professionals, patients and relatives, the qualitative analysis provides a detailed picture of existing services. Illustrations of the current COPD pathway and sub-processes within the pathway are provided, identifying patient, information, resource and emotional flows. Where appropriate we include extracts from the anonymised interview and focus group data.

The research question this study aims to address is whether lean, agile and leagility can be employed to improve the design of patient pathways. The specific objectives for this case research are to:

1. understand how the existing COPD pathway is operationalised; and
2. assess how standardised (lean) and person-centred care (agile) can be employed in the design and delivery of COPD healthcare services.

Chronic Obstructive Pulmonary Disease

"Chronic obstructive pulmonary disease" is an umbrella term used to describe progressive lung diseases which make it difficult to breathe, including emphysema and chronic bronchitis. COPD is a major health problem and a significant cause of premature death in the UK. In England it is the second highest cause of emergency admissions to hospital. COPD accounts for 30,000 deaths per year, 1.4 million general practitioner (GP) consultations, and one in eight emergency admissions—therefore one of the costliest inpatient conditions treated by the NHS, accounting for nearly 10% of all bed days (NICE 2011). Patients experiencing exacerbations commonly seek medical attention late, resulting in hospital admission (preventable if treated early).

The majority of routine COPD care management takes place in primary care, with the most cost-effective interventions being smoking cessation, flu immunisation and pulmonary rehabilitation (PR) (London Respiratory Team 2012).

Pulmonary rehabilitation is reported to be an effective intervention for COPD, with evidence of improvements in exercise capacity, health-related quality of life and dyspnoea (Lacasse et al. 2006). There is also evidence of reductions in length of hospital admissions (Griffith et al. 2000). It is recommended that rehabilitation should be considered at all stages of COPD when symptoms or disability is present (usually Medical Research Council dyspnoea grade 3).

Thematic Analysis of Data

As a result of the thematic analysis of the participant interviews and focus group data, five key themes emerged: pathway architecture, patient flow, information flow, resource flow and emotional flows. Sub-themes were also identified within some of these themes. The analysis and discussion of the data are presented within the five themes.

Architecture of the COPD Pathway

This qualitative study has tracked COPD patients from pre-diagnosis to post-diagnosis crossing a network of services in primary and secondary care. The preliminary results were validated with patients and relatives attending three Breathe Easy groups (groups run by patients for patients and usually supported by the BLF). Four post-take ward rounds were observed on various days and months of the year, including a bank holiday weekend. From analysing the data a high-level process map has been produced which visualises the patient and information flows (see Fig. 7.1) and was used to help identify where lean and agile principles might be applied. The map tracks the patient journey from GP referral through to managing care in the community. Two prominent areas emerged within the pathway which were the pulmonary rehabilitation programme and exacerbations which could result in the patient being hospitalised. From the analysis we propose that at a high level the design of the front-end of the pathway could lend itself to lean principles and the latter parts of the pathway needs to be more responsive to the individual needs of the patients (see Fig. 7.1).

We will further explore the details of the map in the following sections.

Definitions of Pathway

Before examining the detail of the process map, it is important here to consider how staff participants perceived the term "patient/care pathway" and thus to clarify precisely what this study is examining. It was evident from the data that the definition of a pathway and use of the term are highly variable across healthcare professional groups. Some refer to documents (e.g. similar to an ICP); others view it more simply as a trajectory of care that is tailored to the needs of the patient. One participant described it as standardising processes and systems, which he considered extremely important to ensure that patients have options of care offered to them. Another staff participant considered it a "wishy-washy" term that covered

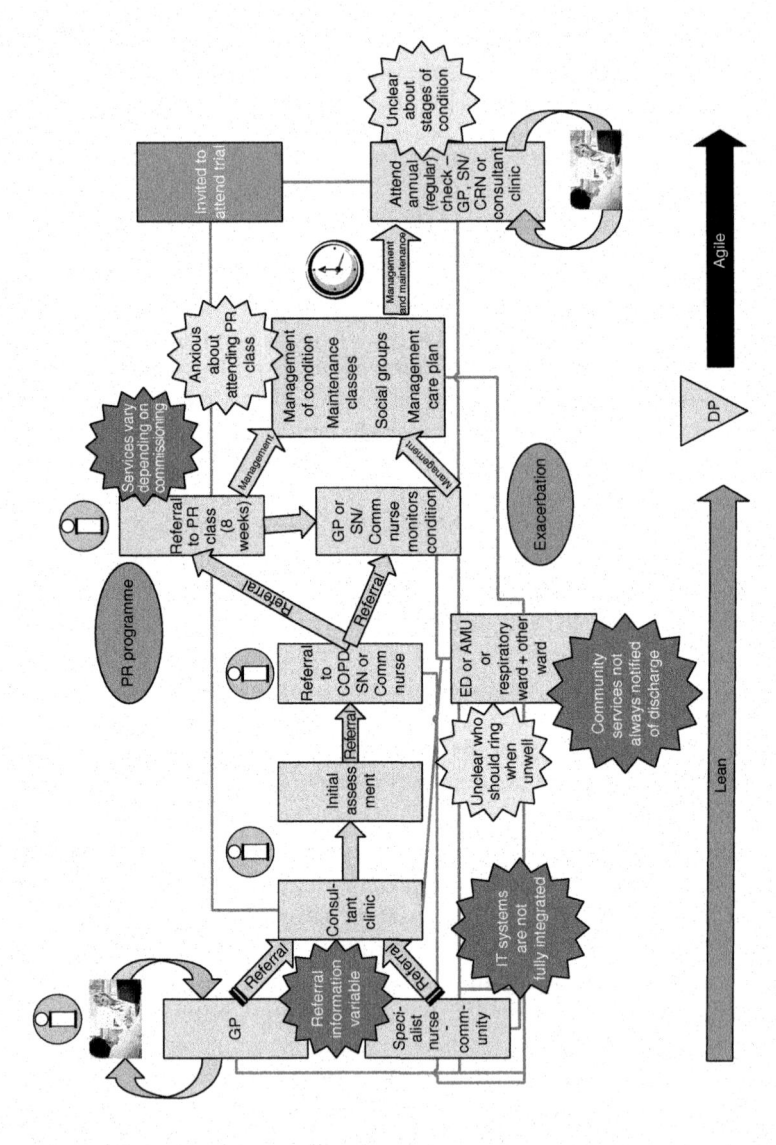

Fig. 7.1 High level of process map of COPD patient pathway. (*Source:* Author)

everything. One participant noted that with the launch of their organisation's new guidelines for the COPD pathway there was more clarity among healthcare professionals around referral criteria to services such as pulmonary rehabilitation (PR). Here we adopt the simple explanation of a trajectory of care that (ideally) is tailored to the patient's condition.

Process Map: Visualising the Pathway
Interestingly when patients were asked to describe their journey most of the discussion was around instances of exacerbations which resulted in a hospital admission or periods when they felt unwell, which suggests the journey is characterised by crisis and its management. Few instances were mentioned where they routinely managed their condition. None of the participants referred to a care management plan and only a few participants mentioned attending maintenance classes. All of the participants recognised the need to remain positive and active if they could. Many talked of their frustration in not being able to do the things that they would like to or had done previously. Coming to terms with being less mobile or active was distressing for some of the participants.

When staff participants were asked to describe the pathway the majority had limited knowledge and were only aware of the services offered by their own team or organisation, unless they had acquired knowledge from working in a different role/organisation. The ability to understand what services are available to patients is accerbated by the different services offered across the different care commissioning groups (CCGs). The staff participants working across these different CCG geographical areas had developed a wealth of local knowledge in relation to what services were available to their patients. When asked about areas of the pathway outside of the services they offered, there was very little understanding of the entire patient pathway, but there was empathy in terms of the complexity of patients/relatives trying to negotiate the various services and people involved in their care.

As a result of the participants descriptions it was possible to construct a generic high-level process map of the pathway (see Fig. 7.1). This is a technique commonly found in the lean paradigm to visualise existing (current state) and ideal (future state) processes/systems.

Critical Points in the Pathway
The process map (see Fig. 7.1) shows several entry points into the COPD pathway. Many of the patient participants recalled having respiratory problems for some time before they were diagnosed. Reflecting on their

journeys some of the patients thought they had had symptoms of COPD long before a clinical diagnosis was given. "... I've probably had COPD for quite a while before it was diagnosed but I think that's quite common, I don't think it's an easy disease to spot...." Similarly, one of the staff participants noted that there had been a few occasions when she had seen patients later in their disease trajectory than she would have liked. She felt that if they had had access to some patients earlier this would have been beneficial to the patient's treatment. One staff participant however noted the difficulty around diagnosis in terms of when this is given and by whom. This can be via the (outpatient) respiratory clinic, from an admission to hospital, or as a result of a referral from another specialist or GP.

The entry point to the pathway may also have had an impact on the patient's understanding of their condition and their response and acceptance of the diagnosis. The referral to the respiratory consultant seems to be a critical point when patients gain a better understanding of their condition and the services available to them. The process for each referral is different and allows for more variance than is needed. Applying lean principles here may help to standardise the information flow and provide greater transparency and management of patient demand within the system and also reduce the possibility of mis- or late diagnosis. Agreement on the information required from referrers needs to be made explicit to minimise any delays.

Attending clinic appointments was viewed by both patient and staff participants as a critical point within the pathway. These usually include routine, evidence-based interventions, such as walking tests and oxygen assessments, which are required before the patient sees the consultant. This suggests greater flexibility is required for the consultation and medication review which need to be customised to each patient. We propose that decoupling at a sub-process level may be used in this part of the pathway. The first part of the appointment may lend itself to lean and the latter part to agility, with the decoupling point (DP) between the assessment and consultation (see Fig. 7.2). The placement of the DP may also

One-to-one assessment — DP — Consultation

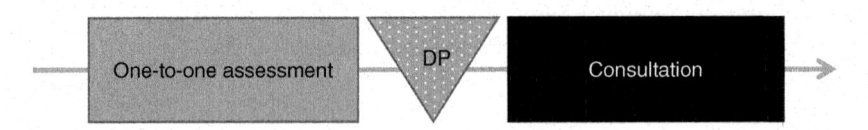

Fig. 7.2 Proposed use of the DP in a sub-COPD process—respiratory clinic. (*Source*: Author)

depend on the severity of the patient's condition. This suggests that scheduling clinic appointments needs to take account of the patient's condition. Allocation of assessments may lend itself to standard times for each patient, but the timing of consultations needs to be more flexible.

Another fundamental part of the COPD pathway is the PR programmes. Typically referrals are received from two sources: consultants (including physiotherapists on the ward and specialist nurses) and GPs (including specialist nurses and practice nurses). All of the patients that had participated in the PR classes spoke positively about their experiences. Exercise plans are tailored to the needs of each patient and their condition. The ability to transfer the exercises undertaken at the class to a home setting was viewed positively by the participants. Some had followed up with the maintenance classes at their local gym but these were not viewed quite as favourable as the PR classes due to the expertise of the PR team not being present. From the data, it would seem that lean principles could be used to streamline the referral process, whereas the flexibility required for the exercise programme may need an agile paradigm.

Care Management in the Community
Post diagnosis, the pathway appears to require a greater degree of flexibility and responsiveness (agility), largely driven by the network of community services, for example, PR and maintenance classes, patients need to access in order to manage their condition. Those patients who had developed good relations with their GP practice and/or have access to specialist community nurses were more positive about taking responsibility for their health. Managing multiple appointments with various healthcare providers was reported by some patients as challenging. Often these appointments were not well coordinated and involved several visits to the same provider in the same week. The lack of integration of the IT systems within and across healthcare systems inhibits some of this coordination. The possibility of patients using hand-held records may help to coordinate their care. Interestingly, some patient participants, with complex conditions, had developed their own excellent (paper based and IT) systems for scheduling appointments, recording changes in medication and reflecting on their general health and well-being.

Decoupling Back-Office and Front-Office Activities
From the high-level map of the pathway (see Fig. 7.1) it is possible to make a distinction between back-office and front-office activities. Given

Table 7.1 Key enablers and inhibitors of patient flow in the COPD pathway

Enablers	Inhibitors
Access to specialist nurses—hospital & community	Not being located on specialist wards
Good access to GP practice—in person or via telephone	Seeing various consultants and other healthcare professionals and needing to continually explain history of condition and symptoms
Diagnosis and procedures clearly communicated to patient/relative	

Source: Author

there are several referral points in the pathway these are likely to be back-office activities (where no face-to-face involvement of the patient is needed). Other activities such as clinic consultations, assessments, PR classes and follow-up appointments are likely to be classified as front-office activities, which rely on contact with the patient.

Patient Flows

The process map (Fig. 7.1) shows the trajectory of care for COPD patients. From the analysis of the interviews and focus groups with patients and staff it has been possible to identify the factors that enable and/or inhibit the flow of patients within the COPD pathway (see Table 7.1).

Information Flows

Frustrations for patients were mainly around the availability and sources of information, which included explanation of their condition, inhaler techniques, and medication. Where opportunities had arisen for patient participants to attend clinical trials they were valued. Tables 7.2 and 7.3 summarise the factors mentioned by patients and staff participants that enabled and inhibited the information flows.

Availability of Information

One patient noted the limited information available when in hospital. As an inpatient he felt he had the time to read this information.

Table 7.2 Factors inhibiting information flows in the COPD pathway

COPD patients/relatives	Healthcare professionals/managers
Lack of information on wards	Lack of integration between IT systems across different healthcare providers
Inadequate explanation of condition	Lack of current information about social care providers
Unclear whom to contact for clarification on changes to medication	Community specialist nurses acquired good local knowledge in relation to service provision across different commissioning groups
Confused about use of inhaler(s)	Some hospital staff unclear what happens in the community and the follow-up care patients receive
Confused about use of oxygen	Frustrating as have to consider what each patient is entitled to depending on where they live
	The healthcare participants based in the community would like a reliable system to notify them when patients are admitted and discharged (if relevant to the COPD condition)

Source: Author

Table 7.3 Factors enabling information flows in the COPD pathway

COPD patients/relatives	Healthcare professionals/managers
Some GP practices have a "flag" system for patients with long-term conditions and complex needs—which enabled them to bypass the usual appointment system and to be seen by a GP or nurse.	Specialist nurses supporting patients in the community as well as following up patients on the wards—continuity of care and transfer of information.
Attending education sessions at the PR classes or social groups such as Breathe Easy.	Community-based specialist team—trying to standardise paperwork across the CCGs. Have considerable local knowledge on what services are available within each area.
Using the Internet to learn more about their condition and join support groups.	

Source: Author

He also wanted to know more about what he could do to help himself manage his condition. Many of the patients had accessed the Internet as a first port of call for information, particularly after their initial diagnosis.

Communication

There was an assumption from the patients interviewed that information would be shared across various healthcare professionals and providers. Seeing different consultants and registrars as an inpatient was often confusing for patients. The need to continually rehearse their symptoms or history was often frustrating. The continuity of care providers in the community was reassuring for patients. Having access to specialist nurses, matrons and/or the same GP was of great benefit for those patients who had this experience. For those that did not they were often at a loss in terms of whom to contact when they were feeling unwell or had a question about the management of their care.

Medication Information

Nearly all participants mentioned their medication and often being unclear as to why changes had been made or if one drug had been changed how this impacted on other medication. Some participants were concerned their medicines had not been checked or reviewed for several years. Another area of confusion for the majority of participants was the use of inhalers. Most referred to them in relation to the colour of the inhaler but seemed to be confused by the differences between each one and why they were using them in the way that they did.

Information Feedback Loops

Feedback loops are a critical part of developing seamless transitions for patients. Referrals and discharge letters are examples of important artefacts which span the boundaries of primary and secondary care. When a patient is admitted to secondary care (hospital) as an outpatient or inpatient this information is needed to update the patient's GP on diagnosis, treatment and changes to medication. Standardising the discharge process, by introducing discharge bundles, has helped to ensure discharge letters are comprehensive and sent in a timely manner. One of the staff participants responsible for completing these letters spoke about the challenge of compiling a letter that was sufficiently informative for the GP and achievable within the limited time frame available, particularly with complex conditions and the pressures surrounding bed availability for in-patient care. It would seem a template for the letter is provided but this is not always completed. This non-compliance suggests either the time and/or availability of information is lacking or there is limited value attached to the letter. Further analysis is needed to map in detail the use of this artefact which appears to be fundamental to spanning the organisational boundaries of secondary and primary care.

Resource Flows

Here we consider the resources required to support patient flow; this could relate to equipment, staff and consumables.

- Access to IT systems
  From the observation of inpatient (hospital) ward rounds there were instances when it was difficult for staff to access computers in order to view patient records. This was particularly an issue if patients were seen whilst in A&E or assessment units.
- Availability of healthcare professionals
  Consistency of staff was an issue raised by some of the patient participants. Seeing the same healthcare professionals is important to patients. They spoke of being able to develop a strong trusting relationship with some key individuals who were consistent in the provision of their care. This was not the case for all participants and often they saw a succession of different staff both in the community and at hospital.
- Access to specialist staff
  Having access to specialist respiratory nurses (primary or secondary care) provided a positive experience in terms of understanding and managing their condition. Not all patients had access to this specialist resource and therefore had a greater reliance on their GP practices.

Emotional Flows

Emotion mapping is described by Johnston et al. (2012, p. 178) as "a simple but powerful extension of journey mapping and it captures the emotions felt by customers as they move through the journey". The authors suggest both negative and positive emotions should be captured and included when improving and redesigning the service. This type of mapping does not tend to feature in quality improvement programmes in industry or healthcare. Yet the sentiments of patients and staff are of significance to us to aid understanding and to identify critical points in the pathway. It is a tool that provides insight to understanding value, expectations and experiences from various perspectives and helps to identify any emotional 'hot spots' that may require additional resource or information. Potentially it is a mechanism to assist in the identification of points in the pathway that need to be more responsive or streamlined.

Below we show two examples from the COPD pathway and the positive and negative emotions reported by patients in the referral process and staff involved in the PR programme (see Figs. 7.3 and 7.4). What is particularly novel in the application of the emotion mapping is the inclusion of staff participants as well as patients. The limited use of emotion mapping until now has focused on customers (patients). We propose this type of mapping is used in conjunction with process mapping activities. It may also be used as one of the feedback mechanisms in relation to the performance of existing pathways.

We discuss the use of emotional mapping, flows and sentiments further in Chaps. 8 and 9.

Discussion

For this case we set two objectives, the first being the need to understand the design and workings of the existing COPD pathway. Here we have provided a high-level map of the general architecture of the pathway. We propose that the diagnosis stage of the pathway lends itself to lean processes. Patient demand data would help to identify any potential for grouping and streaming of patients. It appears at present that the diagnosis and initial assessment is based on a "one size fits all" approach. Further analysis of patient data would enable subtleties of patient conditions to be identified and grouped accordingly. This would enable the runner, repeater and stranger (RRS) categorisation to be employed and sub-streams be identified within the COPD pathway, for example, identifying specific criteria for the RRS categories. This analysis would enable a greater degree of flexibility to be introduced for the stranger category.

The second objective focused on the assessment of how standardised and person-centred care could be employed within the COPD services. From the high-level map and analysis of the participant data we have proposed lean and agile have a role to play in the delivery of COPD services across primary and secondary care. Typically, the pathway design requires greater flexibility when patients are in the community. Healthcare

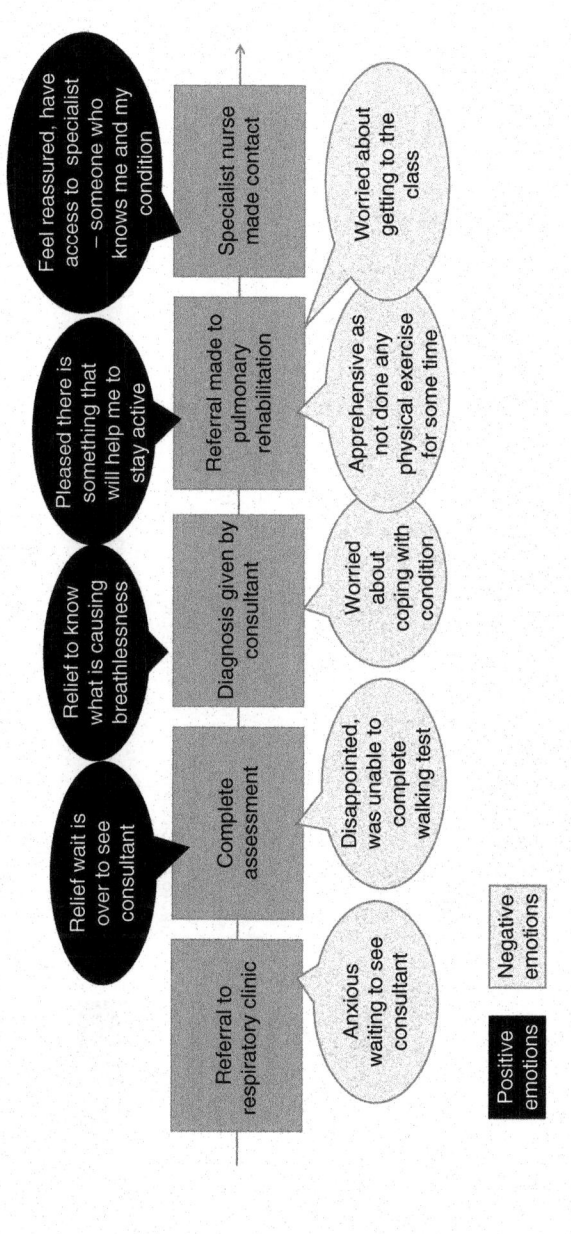

Fig. 7.3 Example of an emotion map for patients. (*Source*: Author)

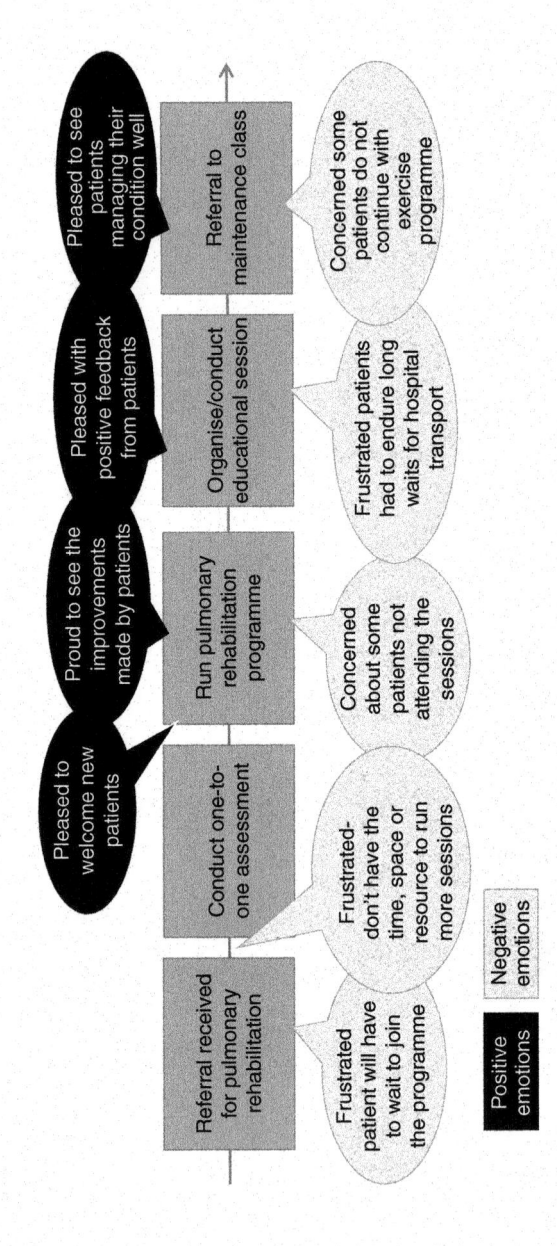

Fig. 7.4 Example of an emotion map for staff. (*Source*: Author)

professionals need to have the information and resources in which to respond to the needs of their patients. We have highlighted examples of where the relevant flows across the pathway are not aligned or are missing altogether. Intervention is required from healthcare professionals, patients and relatives to ensure that the flows are in the right place at the right time. Improved and better integrated IT systems across the entire pathway may help to improve all the pathway flows analysed and discussed above. Fig. 7.1. shows the possible positioning of the decoupling point (DP) where the pathway design needs to shift from a standardised approach to introducing greater flexibility and responsiveness to the individual needs of the patient.

Conclusions

We have demonstrated the applicability of lean and agile at a pathway level and within a sub-process (e.g. consultation clinic). The high-level process map produced here is based on the experiences of patients and healthcare professionals. We propose the referral and diagnosis parts of the pathway lend themselves to standardisation (lean) to ensure that patients receive their diagnosis in a timely and consistent manner. Understanding the level of demand and variation would be of additional benefit here to help with grouping of patients with similar conditions or severity of symptoms for clinics. Alternatively if this is difficult to achieve then understanding how this impacts on scheduling of clinic time must be considered.

The follow-up care is to some extent dependent on commissioning and availability of services. This part of the pathway needs greater flexibility (agile) and person-centredness where patients and their community-based healthcare professionals access the network of services available to them. Often this is more about the seamless transition of the information to ensure that the care is delivered at the right time, in the right place by the right person.

References

Griffiths, T., Burr, M., Campbell, I., Lewis-Jenkins, V., Mullins, J., Shiels, K., Turner-Lawlor, P., Payne, N., Newcombe, R., Lonescu, A., Thomas, J., & Tunbridgea, J. (2000). Results at 1 year of outpatient multidisciplinary pulmonary rehabilitation: A randomised controlled trial. *Lancet, 355*(9211), 362–368.

London Respiratory Team. (2012). Annual report 2011-2012. Cited in Hull, S., Mathur, R., Lloyd-Owen, S., Round, T., & Robson, J. (2014). Improving outcomes for people with COPD by developing networks of general practices:

Evaluation of a quality improvement project in east London. *NPJ Primary Care Respiratory Medicine*, *24*(14082). DOI: 10.1038/npjpcrm.2014.82. Published online 16 October 2014.

Johnston, R., Clark, G., & Shulver, M. (2012). *Service operations management: Improving service delivery* (4th edition). Harlow, Essex: Pearson Education Limited.

Lacasse, Y., Goldstein, R., Lasserson, T. J., & Martin, S. (2006). *Pulmonary rehabilitation for chronic obstructive pulmonary disease (Review)*. London: Cochrane Database for Systematic Reviews.

National Institute for Health and Clinical Excellence (NICE). (2011). *Management of chronic obstructive pulmonary disease in adults in primary and secondary care*. London: NICE.

CHAPTER 8

Analysis of the Huntington's Disease Pathway: Lean, Agility and Leagility

Abstract This chapter presents case research on the design of a patient pathway for a chronic condition Huntington's disease (HD). The case draws on the design of two different services delivered in the UK. From interviewing healthcare professionals, patients and relatives, the qualitative analysis provides a detailed review of existing services. We provide a high-level map of HD pathway which includes details of patient, information and emotional flows. We introduce the theme of brokering and how this fits with the role of the patient, relatives and healthcare professional. We identify how lean and agile influence or might improve the design of the pathway being studied. We propose how the use of decoupling might improve the performance of the pathway including front-office and back-office activities.

Keywords Pathway · Patient · Huntington's disease · Flow · Lean · Agile

INTRODUCTION

This chapter presents the second case study, the design of the HD pathway—described by one of the participants as "family-centred care". The case draws on the design of two different services delivered in the UK but both being centred around a multi-disciplinary model of care. From interviewing healthcare professionals, patients and relatives, the qualitative analysis provides a detailed review of existing services. Where appropriate we include

© The Author(s) 2017
S.J. Williams, *Improving Healthcare Operations*,
DOI 10.1007/978-3-319-46913-3_8

extracts from the anonymised interview data. An illustration of the HD pathway is provided which includes details of patient, information and emotional flows.

As in the previous chapter, the key aim this study sets out to address is whether lean, agile and leagility can be employed to improve the design of patient pathways.

The specific objectives of this case research are to:

1. understand how the existing HD pathway is designed and operationalised; and
2. assess how lean and agile can be employed in the design and delivery of HD services.

Huntington's Disease Pathway

Huntington's disease (HD) is a genetic neurodegenerative disease and is characterised by motor disorder, emotional changes and cognitive decline. Prevalence of HD in the UK is estimated to be one in 10,000 (Evans et al. 2013). The onset of the disease usually happens in mid-adulthood and the neurological decline takes place over a 15- to 20-year period after the initial onset of the symptoms (Dale et al. 2014). Unfortunately, at present, there is no treatment available to slow or prevent the progression of the disease, but a number of potential disease-modifying treatments are under development (Tabizi et al. 2013).

Thematic Analysis of Data

As a result of the thematic analysis of the interview data six key themes emerged: pathway architecture; from person-centred care to family-centred care, patient flow; information flow; resource flow; emotional flows; and co-production of care. Sub-themes were also identified. The analysis and discussion of the data are presented within these key themes.

Architecture of the HD Patient Pathway

Previous HD research has focused largely on clinical and education interventions. There is little research that examines the architecture of the HD care pathway. The design of the pathway will depend on how services are commissioned. In some areas of the UK services involve multidisciplinary teams and in others it is reliant on a specialist nurse who makes referrals into other services. Many HD patients are highly dependent on family members, who may also be at risk of inheriting the disease and/or have children/siblings who are at risk of HD.

Similar to the COPD case study, the fieldwork for the HD pathway included experience-based interviews with healthcare professionals, patient and relatives/carers. As a result, a high-level process map has been produced (see Fig. 8.1), which illustrates a generic pathway, where patients are supported by a community-based multidisciplinary team. We know that this provision is not universal across the UK, which may impact on the likelihood of being able to generalise to other forms of provision; however, we decided to focus our discussion here to demonstrate the benefits this model of care brings to patients and relatives and to offer insight to how this might be improved further.

After the initial stage of diagnosis, the progression of the disease and the type of interventions required will vary for each patient. Interventions are likely to focus on mental health, cognitive/emotional and motor symptoms. The process map, constructed from analysing the interview data, shows the patient trajectory according to how care is organised and the flow of information required to inform all relevant stakeholders.

The pathway focuses on a family-centred service where interventions are "customised" to the needs of the patient and often extends to relatives. This is not to say there is an unlimited offering of interventions, but these are initiated as and when required. In other words, there is not a prescribed list of standard interventions or activities such as you might see in other less complex care pathways (e.g. day case surgery) where the patient demand and condition is more predictable. A recent study evaluated an intervention designed to assist carers of HD patients in developing their knowledge base and methods for coping with the symptoms of HD. In addition to the reported increase in knowledge of, and confidence in their ability to care for HD sufferers, the carers identified three areas of the intervention to be beneficial. First they valued the practical advice received during the intervention and the information provided on coping strategies for carers. Second, there were the benefits of spending time with other carers, and the third were the benefits of being involved in the group discussions included in the intervention (Dale et al. 2014).

98 IMPROVING HEALTHCARE OPERATIONS

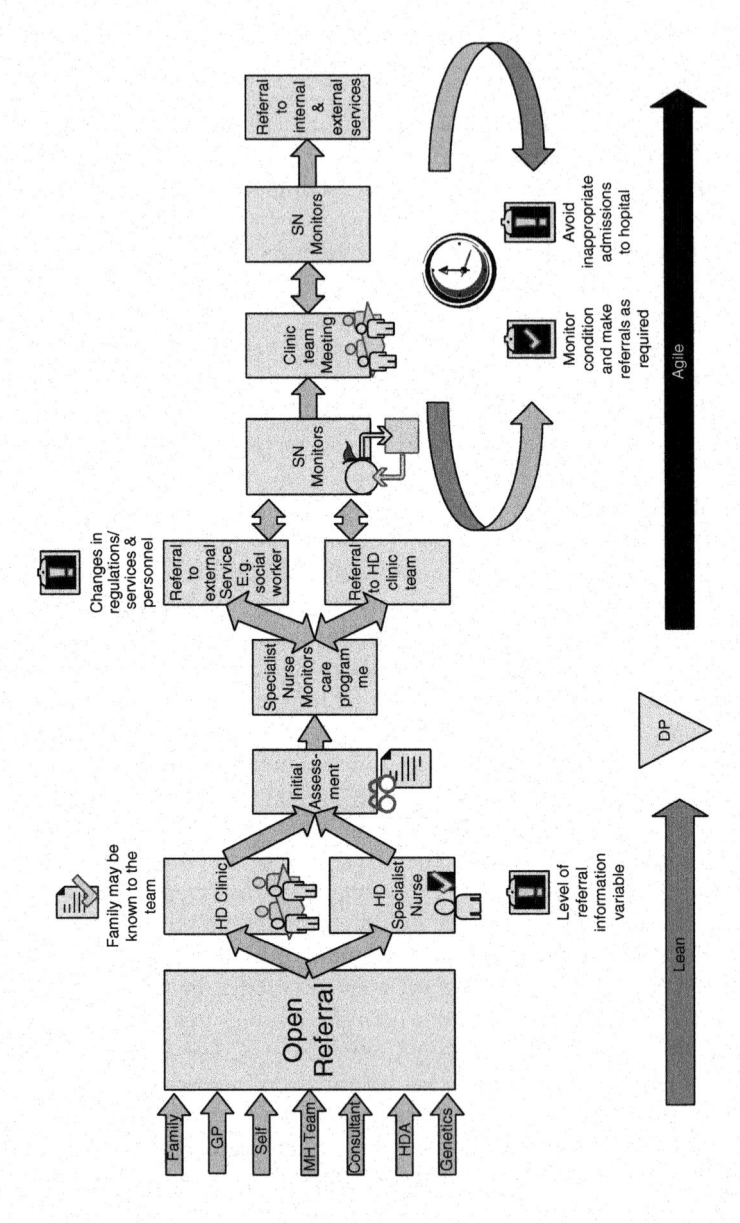

Fig. 8.1 High level of map of HD patient pathway. (*Source*: Author)

Lean and the HD Pathway

Similar to the COPD pathway, it is the first part of the HD care pathway which formulates the referral process that appears to lend itself to lean principles. This may be achieved by the referral template consistently being employed by all referrers in order to standardise and improve the information flow. This may enable the HD teams to process referrals more effectively and efficiently and allocate resources appropriately. Currently, referrals are received in various formats and often information is missing. The referral process appears to be a critical point in the care pathway as it is the activity that the team use to identify the care coordinator and the initial interventions. Once a referral has been received by the HD team it is anticipated that the first assessment is generic and can be conducted by any member of the team. This enables the team to be flexible in allocating care coordinators. The focus here is on processing referrals and to initiate the appropriate provision of care and support required.

Unlike the COPD pathway where there is a high volume of patients being treated, HD is a rare condition and General Practitioners (GPs) and other healthcare professionals making referrals may have limited experience of the disease. The challenge is to ensure the referral is channelled to the right team with right information. In operations management parlance we might term this as a "stranger" condition in that GPs rarely come across the condition. This is different from the high volume of COPD patients seen frequently, which would be termed "runners" or "repeaters". Classifying products and services enables the value streams/supply chains, or in this case patient care pathways, to be designed specifically to meet the individualised needs of the customer/ patient. As the information and knowledge of the patient group develops then the architecture of the pathway can be redesigned to ensure the common elements of care accessed by all patients are standardised and other requirements are individualised depending on the needs of each patient. It is this intelligence of pathway design that needs to be supported by patient data and the knowledge and reflections of the care teams. Patients and relatives also should be central to the redesign of patient pathways.

Agility and the HD Pathway

After the initial core assessment interventions will be "customised" to the needs of the patient. The appropriate therapies and interventions will be made available to the patient. Internal referrals are made among the members of the multi-disciplinary team (e.g. occupational therapist, speech and language therapist, psychologist, specialist nurse, physiotherapist). Staff participants reported there was no defined pattern or pathway and only by putting the patient at the centre of their discussions and reviews were they able to identify his/her needs.

Decoupling Back-Office and Front-Office Activities

From the high-level map of the pathway (see Fig. 8.1) it is possible to make a distinction between back-office and front-office activities. The activities upstream of the MDT meeting are back-office activities which are conducted away from the patient. These include review of referrals, assessment of patient information and allocation of care coordinator. Downstream are the front-office activities which include the one-to-one core assessment, which may well be the first point of contact with the patient and family, along with specialist interventions and assistance with negotiating other providers of care (see Fig. 8.2). In the literature the back-office activities are reported to be where improvements can be made by using lean principles.

From Person-Centred Care to Family-Centred Care

The interest in person-centred care (or similar phrases such as "user-centred", "patient-centred") has gathered momentum, particularly in relation to quality improvement and the design of healthcare services. As HD is a genetic disorder it is possible that family members have already cared for

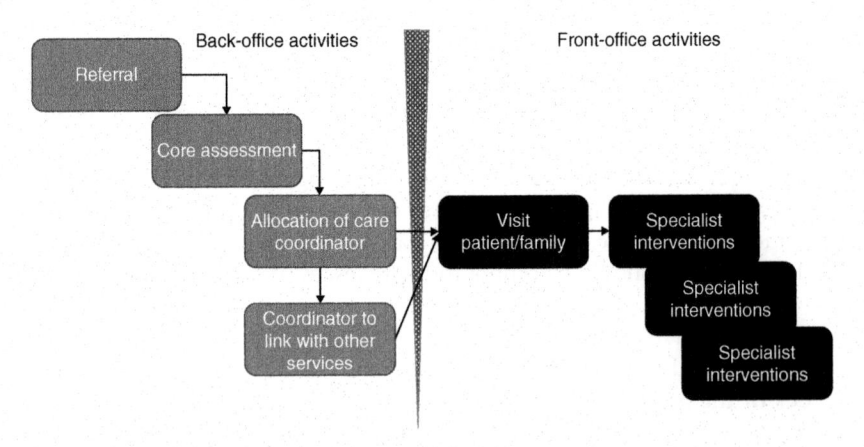

Fig. 8.2 Back-office and front-office decoupling point for HD pathway. (*Source*: Author)

and possibly lost relatives to the disease, hence, some participants described the need for care to be family-centred, rather than patient-centred in order to accommodate the wider social issues of HD. The staff participants spoke about how it was vital to work with members of the family as well as the patient. The well-being of the carers was of particular importance to both the team as well as the patient.

Information Flows

Communication and information were less of an issue for HD participants than those reported earlier for COPD patients. All patients and relatives reported the HD team as being their first port of call should they need any information. As noted above, this might not be directly related to the patient's medical condition, but could have an impact on the general well-being of the patient or the family, for example, issues related to housing, benefits, transport and welfare.

Role of the Broker

The role of the broker was a theme which emerged from both COPD and HD participants, but we have chosen to present it here to limit duplication. Information technology systems within healthcare are often fragmented and healthcare professionals may find they cannot access patient information from outside of their organisation, particularly out of general practice opening hours. In order to bridge this gap there is a reliance on the patient and/or relative/carer to intermediate between the two providers to provide the history and relevant information. Depending on where and why the patient has been admitted this may well affect the flow of information across the care supply chain, for example, if the patient is not treated at his/her local hospital or if new to the area. It is possible that the patient/relative will need to take the role of the broker to ensure the information is available to hospital admission teams and/or community services.

One member of the HD team confirmed the reliance on family members to inform the team when one of their patients is admitted to hospital: "...more often than not the family, very rarely the hospital will ring because... the patient wouldn't say to contact us, they're just in and that's it".

Examples of healthcare participants occupying this brokering role usually involved specialist nurses within the hospital (e.g. respiratory, neurological) who linked with the community services or where community nurse specialists had an in-reach arrangement or good links with the hospital to ensure systems were in place to safely and robustly transfer the necessary information. The initiation of such arrangements appeared to rely on personal relationships that had developed over a period of time or as a result of individuals having previously worked together. If patients were admitted to non-specialist wards, then the brokering role was more likely to be needed. We discuss the implications of this brokering role in Chap. 9.

Emotional Flows

The majority of staff participants commented on frustrations with the wider system, particularly when making referrals to services that had limited understanding of HD: "...sometimes clients get into a muddle, or you can't get colleagues to be as helpful as you would like them to be, from other professions. And I think that's a little bit frustrating sometimes. And you don't have perhaps enough time to go and do all the PR stuff with them."

Staff participants also spoke about the frustrations in relation to not having sufficient time—in particular the time to review the way services are delivered and how these might be improved. "...I think the frustration is having the time to do the other things...We'd like to actually get focus groups together for our clients and just hear their voices again..."

Similarly, patient and relative participants' frustrations were associated with accessing services for additional support outside of that which is provided by the HD teams. One patient spoke of a one-year struggle to access benefits which he and his carer found extremely distressing.

Resource Flow

All of the patient and relative participants spoke positively about the support they received from the MDT. Frequent team meetings enable patients' needs to be reviewed regularly and internal referrals to be made.

The healthcare professionals spoke about the benefits of working in an MDT. The ability to easily communicate with team members and seek advice was one of the main advantages. The generic skills acquired from undertaking the initial core assessments complemented the professional skills of the team members. Additional skills had also been developed in assisting patients and relatives to access other services such as education, social services, welfare, transport and housing.

Co-production of Care

One of the HD teams participating in this research had introduced a patient and relative support group. This monthly meeting was organised by the team, whilst providing an opportunity for patients and relatives to help design the meetings and to choose topics of discussion that were important to them. Relative participants who attended the meetings reported them to be a safe environment in which to share experiences (positive and negative), learn about new or existing support services, and meet others touched by HD. One participant described the meeting, "It's friendly. It's a laugh... You can laugh at your own, some of the things they do without being told, oh that's terrible, you shouldn't laugh! You can actually see the funny side in things... and not feel guilty about it... because they're not going to judge you because they know what you're going through. And they know that you know someone else has been through it too...."

DISCUSSION

The two objectives for this case were to understand how the existing HD pathway is operationalised and to assess how lean and agile can be employed in the design and delivery of HD services. The multidisciplinarity of the HD teams was one of the key factors of the patient care pathway observed as part of this case research. Being flexible and responsive to the needs of the patient and their family/carers was central to design and delivery of the HP pathway. The flow of information and resource is, as for the COPD pathway, critical to the continuity of care and for resources being in the right place at the right time. Emotion flows provided an extra dimension to the usual mapping of information and material flows. Given HD was described as being family-centred we feel the inclusion of emotion flows (both positive and negative) for chronic long-term diseases is crucial.

The flow of information appeared to be critical to the continuity of care and supporting the development of an integrated care system. The brokering role that emerged from these findings is something that requires further attention and possibly resource in the absence of well-integrated IT systems. At the moment this role appears to be administered in an informal way and is dependent on family members or specialist healthcare professionals to identify the point when they need to intervene. Sometimes this intervention is to broker a disconnected system across organisational or functional boundaries. In other instances this is to decouple the system in order to respond to the changing needs of the patient (e.g. when healthcare professionals broker the relationship between the patient and other services—social services, housing, education, etc.).

Here we have presented another type of decoupling—front- and back-office decoupling. Clearly with the latter these can be prepared or completed without the patient being present. It would seem that the majority of the information required to process referrals and allocate care coordinators may be processed without patients being present. This part of the process may be improved by employing lean thinking to remove any non-value adding activities (Guimarâes and Carvalho 2013). In order to increase the efficiency of the pathway it may be possible to identify some front-office activities to be moved to become back office (i.e. do not require interaction with the patient/relative) (Chase and Tansik 1983).

Conclusions

Here we have analysed the design of the HD pathway in relation to pathway architecture, along with information, emotion and resource flows. From the analysis emerged additional but related topics of discussion including the decoupling of front-and-back activities, role of the broker and working beyond the boundaries of the healthcare system. Although this analysis is based upon the HD pathway some of these findings can be generalised to other conditions. The poignant message from this part of the analysis is the need for family-centred care. A multi-disciplinary team, which is well resourced, is one of the key requirements to deliver this model of care. There is also a reliance on the development of local knowledge by the team members of the service provision outside of healthcare that their patients need to access. Here we have looked at the pathway only within the sphere of healthcare—primary and secondary; there is clearly a need to expand this research to health and social care and probably beyond.

References

Chase, R., & Tansik, D. (1983). The customer contact model for organisation design. *Management Science*, 29(9), 1037–1050.

Dale, M., Freire-Patino, D., & Matthews, H. (2014). Caring with confidence for Huntington's disease. *Social Care and Neurodisability*, 5(4), 191–200.

Evans, S., Douglas, I., Rawlins, M., Wexler, N., Tabrizi, S., & Smeeth, L. (2013). Prevalence of adult Huntington's disease in the UK based on diagnoses recorded in general practice records. *Journal of Neurology, Neurosurgery & Psychiatry, 84*(10), 1156–1160.

Guimarães, C., & Carvalho, J. (2013). Strategic outsourcing: A lean tool of healthcare supply chain management. *Strategic Outsourcing: An International Journal, 6*(2), 138–166.

Tabrizi, S., Scahill, R., Owen, G., Durr, A., Leavitt, B., Roos, R., et al. (2013). Predictors of phenotypic progression and disease onset in premanifest and early-stage Huntington's disease in the TRACK-HD study: Analysis of 36-month observational data. *The Lancet Neurology, 12*(7), 637–649.

CHAPTER 9

Discussion and Theoretical Reflections

Abstract This chapter considers the findings of two patient pathway cases in relation to design and improvement paradigms: lean, agile and leagility. We discuss the qualitative results in relation to three theoretical domains: supply chain management, quality improvement and systems thinking. We explore the importance of emotional mapping when improving healthcare services, along with the application of decoupling points (DPs) and brokering roles. We examine the learning in relation to pathway architecture and the contributions made to understanding how lean, agile and leagility may be operationalised in healthcare. As a result of this research we identify key characteristics required to support and develop a sustainable and integrated healthcare system.

Keywords Lean · Agile · Leagility · Quality improvement · Healthcare · Pathway

Introduction

The aims of this study are to understand how the existing chronic obstructive pulmonary disease (COPD) and Huntington's disease (HD) pathways have been operationalised and to assess how lean and agile may be employed in the design and delivery of these healthcare services. Here we discuss the analysis of the two cases presented in Chaps. 7 and 8 in relation to relevant theoretical lenses. We examine the learning with regard to pathway architecture and the contributions made to understanding how lean, agile and leagility may be operationalised in healthcare as advocated by Naim and Gosling (2011).

Pathway Architecture

There is limited opportunity for healthcare professionals to redesign services from a whole system perspective. Many services operate on a 24/7 basis; therefore healthcare does not have the luxury of being able to "stop the line" as in manufacturing. Hence, this has led to point of care and/or project-based improvements being implemented (Burgess and Radnor 2013; Dixon-Woods and Martin 2016). This often results in optimising one part of the process but sub-optimising other parts or in fact the whole system. Taking a systems view early on in the pathway design would be beneficial. Once operationalised, the pathway can then be continually monitored and revised using improvement models and cycles (e.g. PDSA).

The ability to recognise where lean and/or agility can be employed within the design of pathways is a skill that has not been well developed in healthcare. Supply chain managers, system designers or their equivalent in healthcare do not seem to exist. Redesign tends to be localised and not well connected to other parts of the system. Therefore, it is difficult to see who takes responsibility for ensuring pathways are designed to deliver the desired outcomes. There is a need for an organisation to take a lead role to ensure that all care providers involved are aware of their role in the pathway both in terms of delivery of care and improving the service. Performance measurements need to be coordinated, congruent and transparent across the entire care pathway. To develop a sustainable and integrated healthcare system we suggest the following are required:

- Collaborative and long-term relationships between key providers which include at the very least health and social care
- Visibility and alignment of performance measures across the healthcare system
- Sophisticated demand management to support redesign of pathways (and sub-processes), categorisation of patients and allocation of resources
- Development of systems thinking and supply chain management skills to take a holistic view of the pathways which stretch across functional and organisational boundaries

- Well-integrated information systems to support those receiving and giving care
- Inclusion of resource and emotion flows in the improvement of activities to provide a wider view of the complexities associated with delivering care for those with chronic long-term conditions and co-morbidities.

LEAN, AGILE AND LEAGILE IN PATHWAY DESIGN

As a result of the case analyses we propose lean and agile attributes are present in the design of both pathways (see Table 9.1).

Described by healthcare participants as the "bread and butter" of respiratory, the COPD pathway needs to accommodate high volumes of patients (e.g. 900,000 patients diagnosed within the UK). The treatment

Table 9.1 Attributes of COPD and HD pathways

Attribute	COPD pathway	HD Pathway
Typical patient group	High volume, low-medium complexity (L)	Low volume, medium-high complexity (A)
Cycle of care	Chronic long-term condition	Chronic long-term condition
	Routine clinics and tests, oxygen assessments, medication reviews	Regular reviews to assess any changes in need/ provision of care
Focus	Reduce avoidable admissions to hospital	Interventions/therapies customised to needs of patient (A)
	Care management plan (L)	Reduce avoidable admissions to hospital
	Quality of care, patient safety, speed of response—especially for exacerbations	Family-centred service (A) Quality of care, patient safety
Demand for services	Relatively predictable (if no co-morbidities) (L)	Unpredictable (A)
Complexity of care pathway	Low/medium (L)	Medium/high (A)
Level of integration between primary and secondary care	Medium Continuity of care	High Extend to social care Continuity of care

Source: Author
Key: (L)—Lean attribute, (A)—Agile attribute

and care when patients are stable could be described as being relatively predictable. The complexity arrives when patients experience exacerbations which are more difficult to predict and often result in them being admitted to hospital. The focus is trying to minimise avoidable hospital admissions and provide continuity of care across healthcare providers.

For the HD pathway it seems that the model of care is less predictable and interventions need to be carefully planned and designed in order to respond to the individual needs of the patient. Although the volume of HD patients (e.g. approximately 6,000 patient in the UK) are considerably lower than for COPD, the complexity of the needs is much higher. The focus again is trying to minimise avoidable hospital admissions and providing an integrated care package which should extend beyond healthcare.

To expand our discussion to include leagility we have summarised and assimilated the key attributes discussed in Chap. 5 to demonstrate how this thinking may be linked with the design and architecture of the two patient pathways. From our analysis we propose the COPD pathway resembles more of a lean and/or leagility architecture (see Fig. 9.1). It would seem from this case research the most uncertainty of the condition is connected with exacerbations. The pulmonary rehabilitation programmes require some individualised exercise programmes but these are compiled from a limited choice of appropriate exercises for respiratory patients.

In contrast, the HD pathway represents more of an agile/leagility architecture (see Fig. 9.2) which reflects the responsiveness required for the unpredictability of the disease trajectory. As noted earlier, it is the referral process that may lend itself to a lean paradigm.

In Chap. 5 we discussed the role of decoupling within the context of supply chain design (see Fig. 5.3). We identified how this decoupling concept can be used within five different product-based supply chains. In Fig. 9.3 based on our analyses we propose where the positioning of the decoupling point (DP) might be located for both case pathways. For HD the DP is located further upstream than required for the COPD pathway indicating a greater degree of uncertainty around the interventions/therapies and referrals to other services.

The literature also considers the DP as a material DP (MDP) and an information DP (IDP) where the customer order meets an internally forecast-driven plan (Banomyong et al. 2008; Towill and Christopher 2002). Given this study is qualitative in nature it is difficult to investigate the relevance of the MDP in the design of the care pathways. It is likely

9 DISCUSSION AND THEORETICAL REFLECTIONS 111

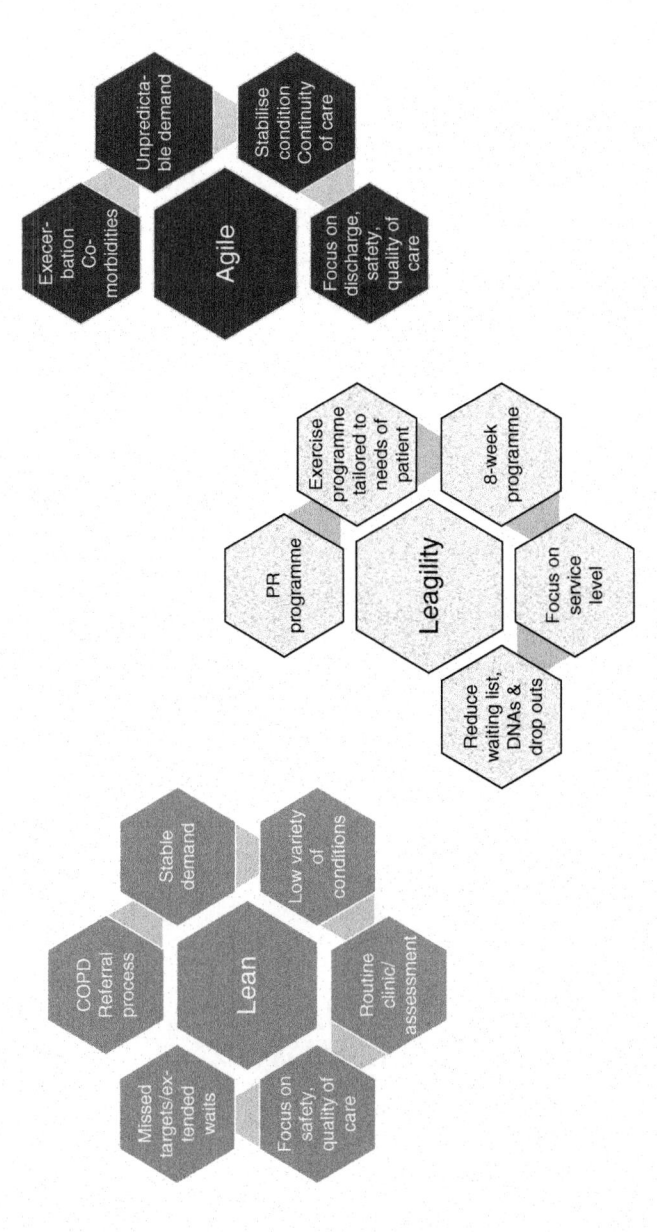

Fig. 9.1 Distinguishing lean, agile and leagility attributes of the COPD pathway. (*Source*: Adapted from Naylor et al. (1999))

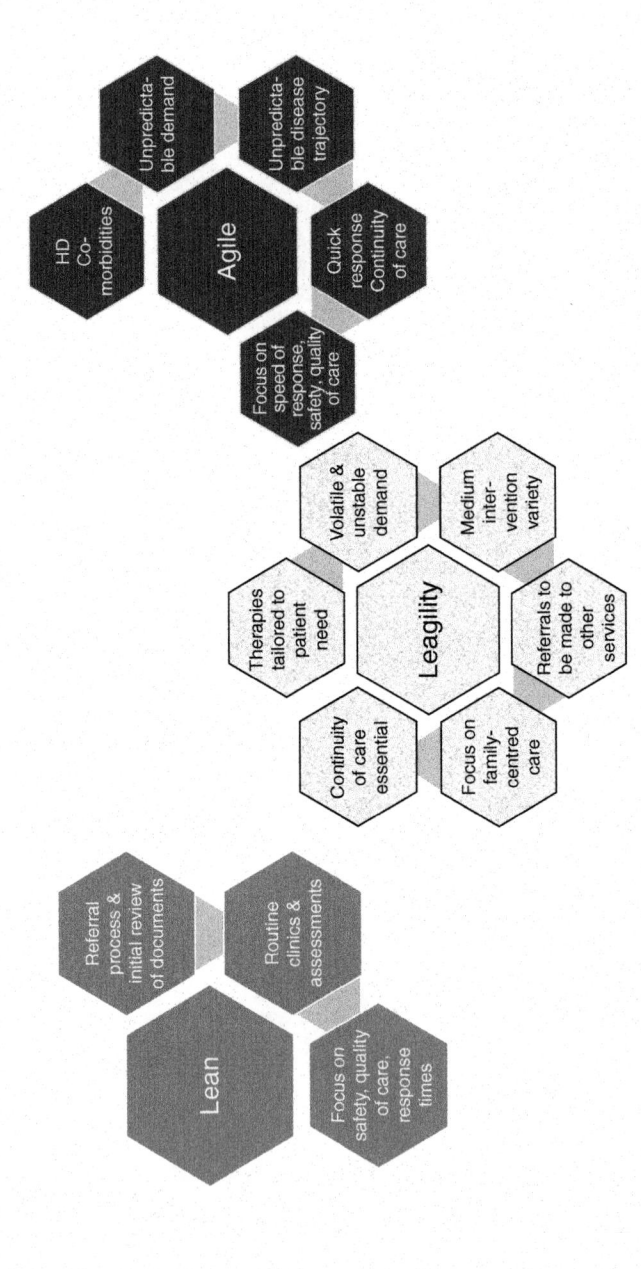

Fig. 9.2 Distinguishing lean, agile and leagility attributes of the HD pathway. (*Source:* Adapted from Naylor et al (1999))

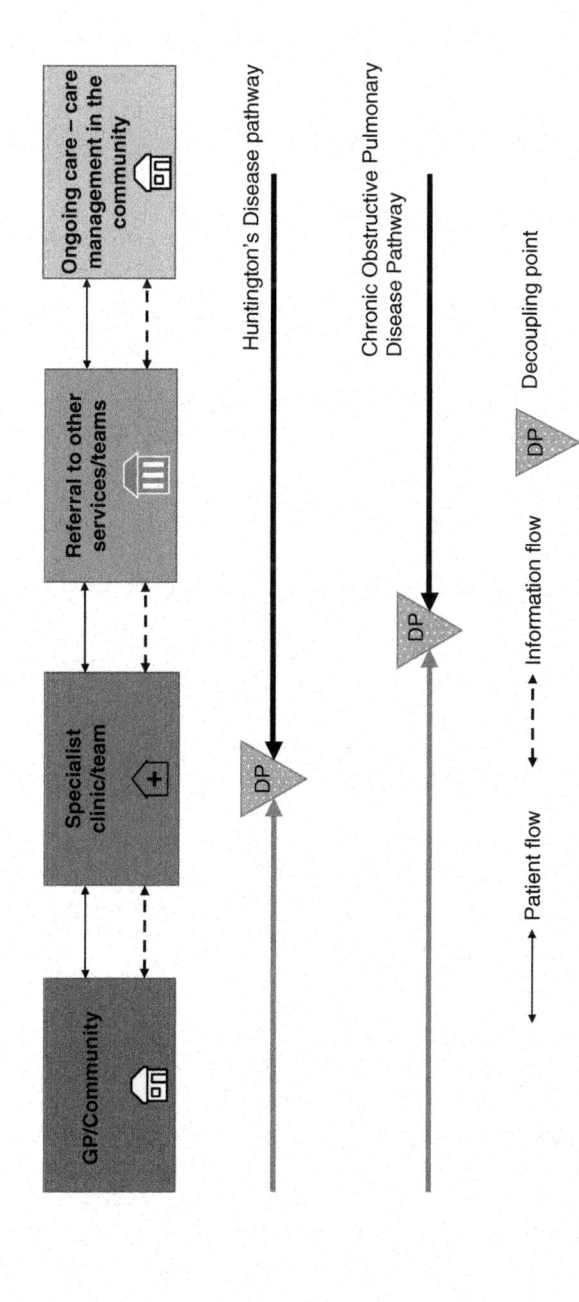

Fig. 9.3 Patient pathways and positioning of decoupling points. (*Source*: Adapted from Naylor et al. (1999))

that this concept could be used for the equipment (e.g. walking aids, wheelchairs, and oxygen cylinders) but quantitative data are needed to understand demand patterns and observational and interview-based studies to understand the current movement of materials in more detail.

Information DPs are probably easier to visualise particularly in relation to referrals and initial assessment of the documentation. Christopher (2000) noted the IDP should be located as far "upstream" in the supply chain as possible to provide details of "real" customer demand. In terms of the pathways this requires not only understanding of the demand patterns of patient referrals but also for the details of the referrals to be accurate and complete. This then enables the respiratory clinics (for COPD patients) and the MDTs (for HD patients) to undertake an initial assessment of the patient needs prior to any face-to-face appointments.

We have considered the decoupling of back-office and front-office activities. This type of decoupling is more straightforward, than perhaps MDPs and IDPs, in its application to a healthcare environment. The literature proposes in order to improve performance, where possible, front-office activities (e.g. those involving contact with patients) are moved to back-office activities (Chase and Tansik 1983). Clearly this might be problematic for some interventions (e.g. physiotherapy, occupational therapy, pulmonary rehabilitation) where contact with the patient is essential. However, with the assistance of technology (e.g. Skype) some of the initial assessments or follow-up consultations may well lend themselves to more of a back-office status.

For this study our discussion on DPs is limited. We have opened up a dialogue on MDPs (equipment, medicine, tests, etc.) and IDPs. We have identified other flows (e.g. resource and emotional flows) which may also lend themselves to the concept of decoupling. Further research and flow analysis is required of patients, emotions and resources to consider what impact these might have on pathway design.

Role of the Brokering Agent

The brokering role that emerged from our analysis is fundamental to achieving service integration. It was evident from the case analysis structural holes or voids (Burt 1992) existed within the pathway which required bridging (Obstfeld 2005) or brokering agents to support the movement of information and sometimes resources (Peng et al. 2010) within the care pathway. These gaps are referred to as structural holes or voids due to the missing links between isolated providers (organisations, functions, specialisms) within the supply network, or in this case patient pathway or healthcare system (Li and Choi 2009; Burt 2005).

It was evident from the interviews with the healthcare professionals, patients and relatives that they all, from time to time, occupied this brokering agent role. Usually this focused on acting as a "buffer" to ensure information was transferred across organisational (external) and functional (internal) boundaries. Healthcare professionals often found themselves acting as boundary spanners as they endeavoured to find information about those patients that had been discharged from hospitals into the community or when a patient had been admitted into hospital. Frequently this relied on the informal "in-reach" or "out-reach" activity that some healthcare professionals had assumed as part of their role. Often the success of such activity was dependent of the relationships developed by the healthcare professionals rather than the healthcare system and/or the design of the pathway.

Patients and relatives also recalled examples of ensuring community healthcare professionals were made aware of hospital admissions. These brokering roles appear to be fundamental to the continuity and integration of care. Further research is required to understand the extent such roles are needed and how reliant existing pathways and systems are on those agents occupying such brokering roles.

Emotional Flows

Emotion mapping is novel to quality improvement in healthcare and is one aspect of this study that is worthy of further theoretical and empirical exploration. This type of mapping develops the process map by including the emotions experienced by customers (patients) at each part of the process or pathway (Johnston et al. 2012). Here we have extended emotion mapping to include patients (customers) and healthcare professionals. It was important to include both perspectives as this provides a more holistic view of the pathway. To our knowledge, this is the first time this type of emotion mapping has been employed as a diagnostic to pathway redesign.

Emotions are often described as strong mental or instinctive feelings, such as pleasure or frustration, delight or disgust (Johnston and Clark 2008). Such emotions may arise due to the tangible benefits and/or the way a customer has been treated. Typically mapping focuses on processes from an organisational point of view. In order to become more focused in our improvement efforts, Johnston and Clark (2008) state there is a need to consider emotions as a key outcome of customer experience. They hailed the need to map the emotions associated with each stage of the process or in this case pathway. Emotions are reported to affect levels of satisfaction. Over three hundred distinct emotions have been identified (see for example Parrott 2001) with the main positive emotions being joy and love, and the main negatives emotions being anger, shame, sadness and fear. Other emotions include surprise, disgust and guilt.

Why we felt it was important to include healthcare professionals, as well as patients, in the mapping of emotion was due to the rate of change expected in healthcare now. Generally conditions in the workplace have undergone considerable change and many workers in the twenty-first century are feeling the strain of working in often chaotic and dysfunctional environments where individuals feel devaluated and discounted altogether (Bergin and Rønnestad 2005). To further develop our conceptual thinking on emotions we briefly draw on the emotional labour literature.

Emotional labour has been described by Brotheridge and Lee (2003, p. 365) as the effort involved when employees "regulate their emotional display in an attempt to meet organisationally-based expectations specific to their role". Whilst many employees want to portray the emotions associated with the display rules, there are likely to be occasions when genuinely felt emotions do not concur with desired emotions (Mann 2005). Emotional labour is debatably perceived to be an important part of the role of many healthcare professionals.

"Perhaps one of the most enduringly popular conceptions of an occupation requiring extensive emotion work is nursing" (Bolton 2001, p. 85). Nurses have been described as the "emotional jugglers" and their ability to face situations that do not necessarily match their feelings (Bolton 2001, p. 86). It was Strauss et al. (1982) who first coined the phrase "sentimental work" in recognition of the emotional component of the role. The changing organisational context and the introduction of concepts such as managerialism and markets mentality have added a new dimension to their work and the need to manage emotions in similar way to those occupying roles in industry. Similarly the patient-centred and coproduction agendas can be associated with the rise in consumerism with patients seeing themselves as consumers with associated rights and expectations.

For many other healthcare professionals emotional labour has not really featured, in particular the medicine profession (e.g. doctors). This is thought to be related to doctors having traditionally been involved in the communication of technical procedures and interventions and leaving the more emotive aspects of caring to nurses (McCreight 2004).

Emotional labour is of considerable importance for those patients who have experienced pain, fear, anxiety and even pain (Phillips 1996). In its simplest form, emotional labour is about maintaining a "cheerful environment" (Mitchell and Smith 2003, p. 114). It has also been described as the "almost invisible bond that the nurse cultivates with the patient". Interestingly emotional labour has not been studied within the realms of quality improvement or pathway redesign. Analysis of the interview and group data revealed critical points where patients, relatives and/or healthcare professionals were frustrated (also known as emotional dissonance (Mann 2005)) with the design of the existing system. It is also important to note there were many positive emotions (known as emotional harmony (Mann 2005)), particularly from patients, that should be recognised in any redesign and improvement activities. Further research is required of this type of mapping to improve how it is integrated with other improvement tools and techniques and explore how it could be methodologically strengthened both in its use and analysis.

Conclusions

In this chapter we provide a synthesis of the main results with regard to the case data presented in Chaps. 7 and 8. The key objectives of the study were to assess how the two pathways have been operationalised and to consider whether lean and agile are present within the architecture and delivery of these services. We propose lean and agile are appropriate paradigms for the design and delivery of these two case pathways. Several themes have emerged within this qualitative analysis which have provided some insights for further research.

The role of the brokering agent is one such area. Further learning from supply chain management will enable us to examine this role in greater detail. The flow of emotion and sentiments is another key finding that is novel within the arenas of quality improvement and supply chain management. Here we have started to investigate how the theoretical lens of emotional labour might add to the analysis of patient and emotion flows.

Here we have responded to the call for further research on leagility in healthcare. Although our study is limited to two patient pathways the findings have provided an empirical insight to how lean, agile and leagility may be operationalised within healthcare and the benefits and challenges these paradigms might bring.

REFERENCES

Banomyong, R., Veerkachen, V., & Supatn, N. (2008). Implementing leagility in reverse logistics channels. *International Journal of Logistics Research and Applications*, *11*(1), 31–47.

Bergin, E., & Rønnestad, M. (2005). Different timetables for change: Understanding processes in reorganizations: A qualitative study in a psychiatric sector in Sweden. *Journal of Health Organization and Management*, *19*(4/5), 355–377.

Bolton, S. (2001). Emotion here, emotion there, emotional organisations everywhere. *Critical Perspectives on Accounting*, *11*, 155–171.

Brotheridge, C., & Lee, R. (2003). Development and validation of the emotional labour scale. *Journal of Occupational and Organisational Psychology*, *76*(3), 365–379.

Burgess, N., & Radnor, Z. (2013). Evaluating lean in healthcare. *International Journal of Health Care Quality Assurance*, *26*(3), 220–235.

Burt, R. S. (1992). *Structural hole*. Cambridge, MA: Harvard Business School Press.

Burt, R. S. (2005). *Brokerage and closure: An introduction to social capital*. Oxford: Open University Press.

Chase, R., & Tansik, D. (1983). The customer contact model for organisation design. *Management Science*, *29*(9), 1037–1050.

Christopher, M. (2000). The Agile supply chain: Competing in volatile markets. *Industrial Marketing Management*, *29*(1), 37–44.

Dixon-Woods, M., & Martin, G. (2016). Does quality improvement improve quality? *Future Hospital Journal*, *3*(3), 191–194.

Johnston, R., & Clark, G. (2008). *Service operations management: Improving service delivery* (3rd edition). Harlow, Essex: Pearson Education Limited.

Johnston, R., Clark, G., & Shulver, M. (2012). *Service operations management: Improving service delivery* (4th edition). Harlow, Essex: Pearson Education Limited.

Li, M., & Choi, T. (2009). Triads in services outsourcing: Bridge, bridge decay and bridge transfer. *Journal of Supply Chain Management*, *45*(3), 27–39.

Mann, S. (2005). A health-care model of emotional labour: An evaluation of the literature and development of a model. *Journal of Health Organisation and Management*, *19*(4/5), 304–317.

McCreight, B. (2004). Perinatal grief and emotional labour: A study of nurses' experiences in gynae wards. *International Journal of Nursing Studies*, 42(4), 439–448.

Mitchell, D., & Smith, P. (2003). Learning from the past: Emotional labour and learning disability nursing. *Journal of Learning Disabilities*, 7(2), 107–117.

Naim, M., & Gosling, J. (2011). On leanness, agility and leagile supply chains. *International Journal of Production Economics*, 131, 342–354.

Obstfeld, D. (2005). Social networks, the Tertius Iungens orientation, the involvement in innovation. *Administrative Science Quarterly*, 50(1), 100–130.

Parrott, G. (2001). *Emotions in social psychology: Essential readings*. Philadelphia: Psychology Press.

Peng, T.-J. A., Lin, N., Martinez, V., & Yu, C. (2010). Managing triads in a military avionics service maintenance network in Taiwan. *International Journal of Operations & Production Management*, 30, 398–422.

Phillips, S. (1996). Labouring the emotions: expanding the remit of nursing work? *Journal of Advanced Nursing*, 24(1), 139–143.

Strauss, A., Fagerhaugh, S., Suczek, B., & Winer, C. (1982). Sentimental work in the technologized hospital. *Sociology of Health and Illness*, 4, 255–278.

Towill, D. R., & Christopher, M. (2002). The supply chain strategy conundrum: To be lean or agile?. *International Journal of Logistics Research and Applications*, 3(3), 299–309.

CHAPTER 10

Conclusion and Future Research Agenda

Abstract This chapter presents a summary of the key findings from this qualitative study which assesses the design of two patient care pathways. We consider the results in relation to the three theoretical lenses introduced in Chap. 2: systems thinking; quality improvement; and supply chain management (SCM). This study is novel in that it examines the application of lean, agile and leagility in the architecture of patient care pathways. We consider what implications the study has for healthcare organisations/practitioners, academics and policy makers. The final part of the chapter offers an agenda for future research for scholars and practitioners interested in healthcare operations management/SCM and integrating healthcare service by improving the design of patient care pathways.

Keywords Lean · Agile · Healthcare · Supply chain · System · Integration

This final chapter presents a summary of the key findings from the study. In particular, it considers the learning from systems thinking, quality improvement and supply chain management (SCM). This study is novel in that it examines the application of lean, agile and leagility in the architecture of patient pathways. The implications of the study are discussed in relation to healthcare organisations/practitioners, academics and policy makers. The final part of the chapter offers an agenda for future research and some concluding reflections on this study.

Linking Theory and Practice

The interest in quality improvement has certainly gathered pace in relation to how we might design and improve the delivery of healthcare services. Many healthcare organisations have embraced various paradigms such as lean thinking to make these improvements. What has been explored less within the healthcare arena is how organisations work with other providers to deliver care across an entire patient pathway. Essentially it is the patient, their carer and/or relatives that see the whole experience. The research has identified the importance of a brokering role which occupies the "structural void" when organisations and systems are not well integrated (Williams et al., 2016). We have noted the importance of sentiments and emotional flows and aligning these and other flows that are likely to be present within a pathway.

We summarise our analysis in relation to the three theoretical lenses which have been focal to this study:

1. Quality improvement in healthcare

As noted previously the efforts around quality improvement have largely been based upon lean thinking. As we have shown here there are many advantages to employing lean to improve healthcare services. However, we have also noted that there are opportunities to use other paradigms such as agility and leagility when more flexibility is required to respond to individual patient/family needs.

There have been calls for more research into how organisations embark on quality improvement and the redesign of services (Dixon-Woods & Martin 2016). It is important for us to understand how organisations decide what approach to take and how these decisions are made. This research has developed our thinking further on how we might integrate different improvement paradigms in order to move away from a 'one size fits all' approach which may not always been suitable for the changes and outcomes we want to achieve.

2. Systems thinking and seamless healthcare systems

We have further developed the conceptual model for a seamless healthcare system proposed by Parnaby and Towill (2008). Through experience-based qualitative data and observations we were able to map the patient pathway for two chronic long-term conditions. The ability to create an integrated healthcare system relies on robust and efficient information systems at all levels within and across the healthcare system. It was evident from both patients and staff participants that these systems where information flows are not always "fit for purpose" and often rely on the intervention of a broker. Further empirical research is required to explore the brokering role for different models of care and healthcare settings and to consider the reliability of such agents.

3. Supply chain management and pathway design

The focus on SCM has largely been limited to architecture and workings of manufacturing-based supply chains. We have drawn on two paradigms: lean and agile to investigate how these might be employed within pathway design. Typically, when we examine the structure and performance of product-related supply chains we are interested in information, material and financial flows. The analysis of two long-term chronic condition pathways has highlighted the importance of patient, information, resource and emotional flows.

We have introduced the concept of leagility to pathway architecture and demonstrated the use of decoupling points (DPs) in the following areas:

- Front- and back-office activities
- Information flows

Further research is required to understand how other the flows we have identified (patient, resource and emotion) might lend themselves to decoupling thinking.

In light of the research we have revised Parnaby and Towill's (ibid) framework (see Fig. 10.1) to reflect a system that spans primary and secondary care. We have included additional tools such as flow analysis and supply chain design practices to improve levels of integration and patient-/family-centred principles have been added in response to the flexibility of care need for some pathways (e.g. Huntington's disease) and the wider coproduction agenda. Further research is required to assess its applicability to delivering seamless healthcare systems.

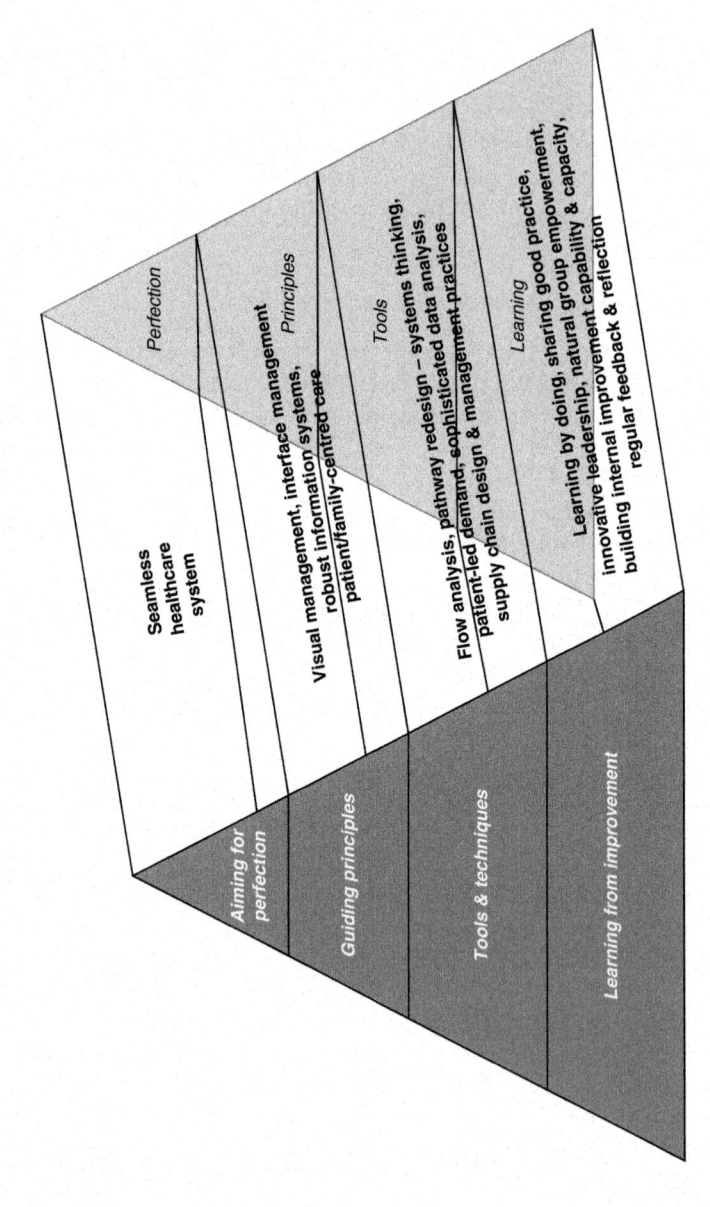

Fig. 10.1 Seamless healthcare system. (*Source*: Adapted from Parnaby and Towill (2008) and Werr et al. (1997))

IMPLICATIONS OF THE RESEARCH

The implications of this study are threefold:

1. Healthcare Organisations and Practitioners

The key message for healthcare professionals and managers involved in the design, delivery and improvement of patient pathways is to challenge the myth of "one size fits all". Integration is fundamental to a seamless healthcare system along with the ability to select the appropriate tools, techniques or approaches in order to achieve the desired outcomes. We have seen an upward trajectory in the use of lean principles in healthcare improvement, but so far agility and leagility have received limited attention. Awareness of these improvement paradigms needs to be heightened among healthcare improvers and educators to enable an integrated approach to be taken when appropriate.

Supply chain management knowledge and skills appears to be limited within healthcare. Organisations in other sectors have recognised their performance is only as good as those companies operating within their supply chain. As a result they have and continue to invest in operations management and supply chain management knowledge and skills. If healthcare organisations are serious about delivering joined up care then a similar investment is needed in equivalent positions that will help develop the partnerships and infrastructure required to deliver integrated healthcare services.

2. Academics

This research has straddled several disciplines and subject areas – (service) operations management, SCM, quality improvement and healthcare management. It has been challenging to manage the complexity of multidisciplinary research and to report the results in a way that is meaningful to different audiences. Cross-disciplinary research needs to have a higher standing in academia. Working in multidisciplinary teams is something we see regularly in our research settings and should feature more in academic institutions and publications. If we are to tackle the challenges alluded to in Chap. 1 then there is no better time for the uniting of the divides of a "specialist" disciplines. Later in the chapter we provide a research agenda which requires academics and healthcare professionals to engage with and take forward.

3. Policy makers

Integration and whole systems thinking has been a common theme throughout this study. We have recognised the importance of joined-up care and witnessed that when systems and organisations are not well aligned the emotions and sentiments this creates for patients and staff. Some of the difficulties around creating a more integrated healthcare system are related to targets and measures being set for individual providers. More attention needs to be given to mechanisms that will support a seamless healthcare system many of which we have discussed here.

Limitations of the Study

This study has its limitations, some of which will serve as the stimulus for future work. Whilst we have examined the design of two care pathways this has limited our study to two long-term conditions. The HD model of care that featured in this study is not universal and therefore may limit the generalisability of the results. Co-morbidities and the fact that some of our patient participants were on more than one care pathway have not been captured. Therefore further research is needed to reflect complexities of different models of care and patient groups.

We have limited our definition to agility to focus largely on a supply chain perspective. We have paid less attention to the agile manufacturing system. Further exploration of this approach would be beneficial to healthcare systems.

The qualitative design of this study has enabled us to provide an insightful account of the experiences of the pathway from staff, patients and relatives. However, quantitative analysis of patient demand patterns would provide further insight, assisting the categorisation of patients and enabling a more sophisticated analysis of the pathway, creating sub-pathways or value streams.

Here we have taken several models and theories which have mainly been tested within a manufacturing environment. At times it has not always been possible to translate the terminology into something meaningful to patient flows and pathway design. Further work is needed to ensure clarity of terms and how these are viewed within the healthcare arena.

Research Agenda

As a result of this research and the consideration of various models and theoretical lenses a number of fundamental points of discussion have arisen which provide an agenda for future research.

1. Here we have examined the *patient pathways* of two long-term conditions and using lean and agile have endeavoured to assess the contribution these approaches can make to a seamless and integrated healthcare system. Further research is required to examine other medical conditions to empirically test the revised conceptual model for a seamless healthcare system as shown below (see Fig. 10.2). We have adapted this model to reflect the complexity of managing and improving end-to-end patient pathways and the processes and sub-processes these are likely to include. Further detail on information, resource, emotion and patient flows have been proposed along with the inclusion of SCM skills and practices. Consideration should also be given as to whether SCM can contribute to improvers developing system thinking habits (Lucas 2015).

    Healthcare systems may not necessarily follow the traditional (manufacturing) approach to leagility, where lean is positioned upstream and agile is located downstream of the DP. Similarly, for those organisations that have embraced lean healthcare, in situations/environments where demand is unpredictable and constantly changing, it might be time to move on to agile healthcare.

2. This research has spanned primary and secondary care. The findings from the HD pathway clearly indicated that our view of *systems thinking* needs to be much wider and engage with other services such as education, welfare, transport and social services. Future research needs to extend our thinking in terms of the healthcare and social care systems to further understand what role lean, agile and leagility can play in "*citizen*" pathways.

3. We have started to investigate here the use of *decoupling* within healthcare. Further research is required to assess demand patterns and analyse the different flows we have identified here (e.g. patient, emotion and resource) to understand whether the positioning of DPs is appropriate to pathway (re)design.

4. *Emotional flows* have been considered within the context of service operations but little research has focused on its use in healthcare

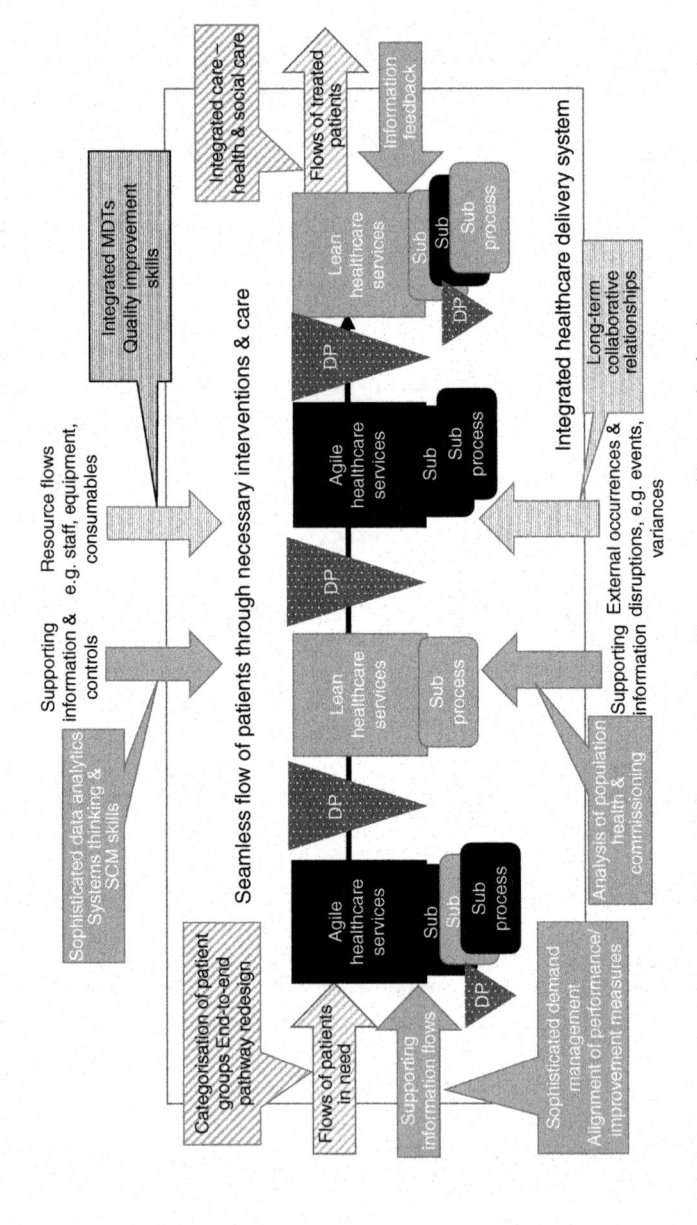

Fig. 10.2 Revised conceptual model for seamless healthcare system. (*Source*: Author)

systems. The experience-based interviews used here have indicated that we need to identify and manage these flows more carefully when looking to redesign or improve services. Both negative and positive sentiments need to be captured within the mapping of pathways. Emotion maps have been used in sociological studies for some time and offer rich analytical rewards. Further research is needed to explore how the emotion map method can be adapted and deployed within various healthcare settings and used with other improvement approaches and methods. Similarly, theory and methods associated with sentiments should also be included.

5. Here we have employed high-level process maps to visualise the patient pathways as experienced by patients and staff. In order to illustrate the various stakeholders involved in the pathway and the interaction between them and the patient we recommend that *service blueprinting* is employed (see for example Radnor et al. 2013). There is limited use of this type of mapping in healthcare improvement yet this is a useful tool. It differs from process mapping in that it simply demonstrates front- and back-office activities and provides greater clarity of stakeholder contributions and line of sight and interaction with patients and relatives.

6. Earlier in this study we briefly introduced *agile methodology*, a project planning tool largely used in the development of software. We feel this paradigm has an important role to play in the redesign and improvement of pathway design. As discussed in Chap. 3, lean healthcare has developed some traction in the improvement of healthcare services. In order to move to agile healthcare, the agile methodology and project planning methods sprint/scrum could be one of the methods used to help develop agile planning and scheduling: facilities planning, human factors, IT systems and supply chains. Linking this methodology with existing models and frameworks such as the model of improvement (see Fig. 4.3) may help to operationlise this novel approach to improving healthcare services.

7. We have taken SCM as one of our theoretical lenses in which to examine the design of patient pathways. It could be argued that this study has adopted a relatively linear (chain) approach to understanding how the pathways have been operationalised. What we know from some of the participant interviews is that parts of the pathway are more complex than perhaps is fully portrayed here. This suggests that the term "supply network" is more fitting to pathway designs

rather than "supply chain". To build on this research and the recommendation made in point 1, it is suggested a *network of pathways* to be used as the unit of analysis for future studies which will help to reflect the journeys of those patients with complex needs and co-morbidities. This may help to move away from the linear connotations that supply (care) chains might bring. We anticipate studying a network of pathways will provide further insight to achieving an integrated health and social care system.

Conclusions

Given the challenges global healthcare systems are facing, quality improvement is likely to remain on the agenda for the foreseeable future. Here we have endeavoured to operationalise supply chain and improvement concepts within the realms of patient pathway design. Specifically, we have examined the architecture of two pathways to identify whether the concepts of lean, agility and leagility could be employed to help improve healthcare systems. Although this study is UK-centric we believe the results are applicable to other public healthcare systems.

The application of lean principles is relatively well established in healthcare. Here we have proposed how agility and leagility may also be included within the toolbox of healthcare improvers. This toolbox recommendation comes with the caveat that improvement programmes are set within the context of the wider healthcare system. The results shared here have repeatedly shown the lack of integration of patient and information flows across the healthcare system. We believe a better understanding of pathway design and the improved understanding of and alignment of flows would help to deliver sustainable change and better experiences for patients, relatives and staff.

As we continue to see the shift of care to the community, there is no better time to take a wider view of our healthcare system. Typically, patient (citizen) pathways cross many service providers in health and social care. Taking a (supply) care network view will help us to see where resources and investment are required in order to deliver the (family) person-centred, well-integrated system that has long been our goal. Here we have taken three theoretical lenses in which to evaluate the architecture of existing patient pathways. Operational excellence remains the goal for healthcare systems universally. Lean healthcare has been on the improvement agenda since the early 2000s (Radnor and Osborne 2013). Is it time to provide the next platform for change – agile healthcare (or leagililty hybrid model) – to help meet the challenges and complexities of a healthcare system in the twenty-first century.

References

Dixon-Woods, M., & Matin, G. (2016). Does quality improvement improve quality? *Future Hospital Journal, 3*(3), 191–194.

Lucas, B. (2015). Getting the improvement habit. *BMJ Quality & Safety*, Published Online First: [30th December 2015]. doi:10.1136/bmjqs-2015-005086.

Parnaby, J., & Towill, D. R. (2008). Seamless healthcare delivery systems. *International Journal of Health Care Quality Assurance, 21*(3), 249–273.

Radnor, Z., & Osborne, S. (2013). Lean: A failed theory for public services? *Public Management Review, 15*(2), 265–287.

Radnor, Z., Osborne, S., Kinder, T., & Mutton, J. (2013). Operationalizing co-production in public services delivery: The contribution of service blueprinting. *Public Management Review, 16*(3), 402–423.

Williams, S.J., Radnor, Z., Aitken, J., & Esain, A. (2016). *Patient-centric and process-centric helathcre supply chains: The role of the broker.* Presented at the 10th International Organisational Behaviour in Healthcare Conference, 5–6 April, Cardiff.

Index

A
A3, 39
Acute, 35, 64
Agile – definition, 10, 46, 47, 53, 58
Agile healthcare, 47, 48, 50, 127, 129, 131
Agile manufacturing, 10, 46–47, 48, 126
Agile methodology, 10, 52, 53, 54, 129
Agile paradigm, 85
Architecture, 10, 40, 55, 66, 81, 90, 96, 104, 108–110, 117, 121, 123, 130

B
Back-office, 62–63, 85, 100, 114, 123, 129
Blueprinting, 129
Broker, 11, 101, 103, 104, 114–115, 117, 122, 123
Brokering role, 101, 102, 103, 114, 115, 122, 123

C
Care commissioning groups (CCGs), 83
Chronic Obstructive Pulmonary Disease (COPD), 8, 22, 70, 71, 79, 80, 107
Clinics, 22, 73, 93, 114
Co-design, 51–52
Collaborative, 33, 48, 108
Communication, 18, 33, 36, 88, 101, 117
Community, 4, 9, 64, 71, 72, 73, 76, 81, 85, 88, 89, 90, 93, 97, 101, 115, 130
Comorbidities, 50, 111, 112
Conceptual model/ framework, 57, 64, 65, 122, 127, 128
Continuous production system, 18
Co-production, 45, 51, 52, 54, 96, 103
Customer, 9, 16, 22, 30–32, 33, 37, 46, 47, 53, 54, 58, 62, 89, 90, 99, 110, 114, 115, 116
Customise, 84, 97, 99

D

Data triangulation, 74
Decoupling, 6, 10, 58, 60–62, 64, 66, 84, 85, 93, 100, 104, 110, 113, 114, 123, 127
Demand management, 108
Deming cycle, 38
Diagnosis, 9, 32, 76, 84, 87, 88, 90, 93, 97
Discrete object manufacture, 18
Disease, 2, 70–71, 84, 96–97, 99, 101, 103, 110
Downstream, 16, 59, 62, 66, 100, 127

E

Emotional flows, 11, 80, 81, 89–90, 96, 102, 114–115, 122, 123, 127
Emotional labour, 116–117
End-consumer, 33, 62
End-to-end, 127
Ethics, 70, 76
Exclusion criteria, 72
Experience-based interviews, 73, 76, 97, 129

F

Family-centred, 95, 97, 100, 104, 123
Flexibility, 10, 40, 45, 46, 53, 54, 84, 85, 90, 93, 122, 123
Focus groups, 73, 74, 79, 86, 102
Forecast-driven, 62, 110
Front-office, 62, 85, 86, 100, 104, 114
Functional boundaries, 103
Functional silos, 19, 36

G

General Practice (GP), 7, 9, 22, 80, 84, 85, 87, 88, 89, 99, 114
Global healthcare systems, 1, 130

H

Holistic, 7, 10, 108, 115
Hospital, 3, 4, 8, 18, 22, 32, 35, 36, 64, 71, 72, 73, 79, 80–81, 83, 84, 86, 88, 89, 101, 110, 115
Huntington's Disease (HD), 8, 11, 70–71, 72, 95–105, 107, 123
Hybrid, 58, 59, 113

I

Inclusion criteria, 72
Information decoupling point (IDP), 62, 110, 114
Information flows, 64, 81, 84, 86–87, 101–102, 123, 130
Information sharing, 32, 33
In-reach, 101, 115
Integrated Care pathway (ICP), 9, 19, 70
Intermediate, 101
Inventory, 32, 62

L

Leagility – definition, 6, 10, 58, 64, 107, 121
Leagility paradigm, 58
Lean – critics, 33–34
Lean – definition, 9, 29–30, 58, 84
Lean healthcare, 35–36, 48, 50, 127, 129, 130
Lean manufacturing, 46
Lean paradigm, 83, 110
Lean principles, 7, 30, 31, 55, 60, 81, 84, 85, 99, 100, 125, 130
Long-term condition(s), 4, 109, 123, 126, 127
Long-term relationships, 108

M

Maintenance classes, 83, 85
Manufacturing, 4, 6, 8, 10, 33, 37, 40, 45, 46, 47, 48, 53, 57, 58, 60, 66, 108, 123, 126, 127
Material decoupling point (MDP), 62, 110, 114
Model of improvement, 52, 55, 129
Models of care, 3, 123, 126
Multi-disciplinary, 95, 99

N

NHS, 1, 3, 7, 8, 32, 33, 55, 70, 76, 80

O

Organisational boundaries, 17, 19, 33, 35, 48, 72, 89, 108
Out-reach, 115

P

Patient-centred, 2, 4, 5, 9, 38, 48, 51, 100, 101, 116
Patient flows, 19, 62, 64, 81, 86, 126, 127
Patient satisfaction, 36–38, 39
Patient trajectory, 9, 97
Performance measures, 108
Person-centred, 2, 34, 45–55, 80, 90, 93, 96, 100, 130
Plan-Do-Study-Act (PDSA), 30, 38–39, 52, 53, 55, 108
Postponement, 62, 64
Primary care, 8, 9, 10, 36, 76, 80, 89
Prism model, 19
Process map, 22, 23, 81, 82, 83, 86, 93, 97, 115, 129
Product-based, 62, 110

Professional silos, 36
Pulmonary rehabilitation (PR), 73, 80, 81, 83, 110, 114

Q

Qualitative research, 69, 74
Quality improvement – definition, 9, 22–24
Queues, 64
Quick-response, 59

R

Readiness, 38, 40
Referral, 81, 83, 84, 85, 86, 88, 90, 93, 97, 99, 100, 102, 104, 110, 114
Resource flow, 81, 89, 96, 102, 104
Runners, Repeaters, Strangers (RRS), 17, 99

S

Safety, 17, 19, 30, 34, 36, 39, 52
Seamless healthcare systems, 17–22, 64, 122–123
Secondary care, 9, 35, 40, 71, 81, 88, 89, 90, 109, 123, 127
Semi-structured interviews, 73, 80
Shewart cycle, 38
Specialisation, 18
Standardisation, 35, 40, 93
Structural void, 122
Sub-processes, 80, 108
Supply chain, 4, 7, 8, 9, 10, 16, 17, 19, 29, 30, 33, 37, 40, 45, 48, 54, 58, 59, 61, 62, 63, 64, 66, 71, 99, 101, 108, 110, 114, 117, 121, 123, 125, 126, 129, 130
Supply chain management, 7, 8, 16–17, 33, 108, 117, 121, 123, 125

Support group, 103
Sustainability, 35, 36
Swift, even flow, 19
Systems engineering, 19
Systems thinking – definition, 9, 11, 16, 17–21, 107, 121, 127

T
Thematic analysis, 73, 74, 76, 81, 96
Toyota production system (TPS), 30
Translation, 37, 48, 66
Transparency, 84

U
Upstream, 16, 59, 62, 66, 100, 110, 114, 127

V
Validation, 74, 80
Value, 6, 9, 16, 17, 24, 31, 32, 33, 34, 36, 37, 38, 39, 40, 46, 51, 52, 54, 60, 86, 88, 90, 97, 99, 104, 126
Variance, 84
Variety, 58, 76
Volume, 17, 47, 58, 60, 70, 71, 76, 99, 109, 110

W
Waiting lists, 64
Ward rounds, 73, 81, 89

Z
Zara, 59, 62

Printed by Printforce, United Kingdom